Contents

Foreword

Every so often there is a book which produces an unusual angle on a particular topic – one that causes you to think in new ways about old issues.

This, I believe, is one of those books. We have had books called *The Self-Managing School* and the *Parent Friendly School* but the *Health-Promoting Primary School* is at the first blush esoteric and a title for a very particular taste. Nothing could be further from the truth.

The book should be on the reading list not only of every would-be teacher but also of every Deputy and Head Teacher. It shows how it is possible from whole school commitment to health issues to proceed to successful teaching and learning within schools. Nothing now is more important than that. As an institution the school was invented by societies as a place to put young people so that they should understand written words and numerical systems. To that was added over the years many responsibilities – all in the field of knowledge. In the last twenty years the other pillars of society – the family and the Church – have declined in influence, especially amongst those in economic disadvantage whom we now chillingly call the 'under class'. There are disproportionate numbers of people in poverty in urban areas and one of the injustices they have to bear is ill-health on a large scale. Our fellow citizens in such areas read the advertisements and pay VAT on cigarettes or drink. Often knowledge in such areas is inadequate. Suddenly it is all too clear that if we are to break the cycle of disadvantage, health promotion must be at the heart of the primary school simply because its importance as an influence in the lives of people has increased as that of the family and Church have declined.

So this book is timely. To those who read it there is the promise of seeing schools and teaching as through glasses which have suddenly brought the familiar into much sharper focus.

Professor Tim Brighouse
Chief Education Officer
Birmingham LEA

The
Health-Promoting
Primary School

Edited by

Ron Morton and John Lloyd

David Fulton Publishers

David Fulton Publishers Ltd
2 Barbon Close, London WC1N 3JX

First published in Great Britain by
David Fulton Publishers 1994

British Library Cataloguing in Publication Data

A catalogue record for this book is available from the British Library

ISBN 1-85346-325-6

Typeset by Harrington & Co.
Printed in Great Britain by BPC Books & Journals Ltd., Exeter

Preface

As Sir Ron Dearing notes in his report on the National Curriculum and its Assessment (1993), 'Education is not concerned only with equipping students with the knowledge and skills they need to earn a living. It must help our young people to use leisure time creatively; have respect for other people, other cultures and other beliefs; become good citizens; think things out for themselves; pursue a healthy lifestyle; and, not least, value themselves and their achievements.'

This book explores the challenges that primary schools face in promoting the health of their pupils and those who live and work in their communities. It reflects upon the context in which schools exist, particularly on the social, political and economic environments which inevitably impact on schools and their communities. Upholding Dearing's statement about pupils 'thinking things out for themselves', suggests that through children's own decision-making, changes can be brought about that promote the health and well-being of individuals and ultimately the communities in which they live.

Each writer raises important questions regarding entitlement and ownership and the need for schools to encourage choice rather than restrict it. Values, priorities, responsibilities and issues of empowerment are addressed to help schools proceed from merely delivering health education to actively promoting the health of its community, with a programme and ethos geared towards people 'valuing themselves and their achievements'.

The health-promoting primary school is one that acknowledges its crucial role within a welfare network. It forms essential alliances and partnerships with parents, governors, pupils, health professionals and the various agencies that serve the health needs of all children. The roles that each play in the promotion of health are key features in this book, being addressed at not only a theoretical and policy level but also at the level of implementation.

It is hoped that all involved in health education and health promotion in the primary school should find here a catalyst to clear thinking and understanding. The chapters encompass educational parameters within health and health parameters within education, by providing the means, through practical activities and experiences, for the school and its community to become effective custodians of their own health and welfare needs.

Contributed chapters reflect the accumulated experience and expertise of practitioners engaged in meeting the day to day demands of health promotion in schools and their communitiies. However, the opinions expressed are solely their own and do not necessarily represent the views of the agencies or authorities for whom they work.

The editors wish to express their gratitude to Jean Willcox for her administrative support and good humour throughout the preparation of this book.

Ron Morton & John Lloyd
Birmingham
July 1994

About the authors

Eileen Bruce

Eileen Bruce is County Co-ordinator for Personal, Social and Health Education and Child Protection for Hereford and Worcestershire Education Department. A trained teacher and health education officer, she has worked in education and health for the last twenty-five years. A lecturer and trainer on a wide range of health issues, she has also contributed to articles on Health Education, Sex Education, Pre-conceptual Care, and Solvent Misuse. An expert counsellor, she has worked with traumatised children and their parents, and other adults.

Kay Danai

Kay Danai is currently a Lecturer in Education at Worcester College of Higher Education. Formerly a class teacher at the Spennells First School, Kidderminster, she was responsible for the development and co-ordination of health education throughout the school. Her research into the initiation and implementation of a health education programme in her school, described in her chapter, formed the basis of a dissertation presented as part of a Master's Degree in Education.

John Lloyd

John Lloyd is a Senior Teacher Consultant with Birmingham LEA Curriculum Support Service, responsible for the development of Cross Curricular Themes. He was a member of the National Curriculum Council Task Group which produced *Guidance 5: Health Education*. Co-author of *Blueprints Health Education, Democracy Then and Now* and *We've Seen People Drinking*, he has worked with TACADE and is a member of RoSPA's National Safety Education Working Group and Brook Centre's Special Publications Advisory Group.

Ron Morton

Ron Morton is Head Teacher of West Heath Junior School, Birmingham. Committed to health education, his school featured in ITV's INSET programme *The Health-Promoting School, Good Health in the Classroom and All My Very Own*; the last being part of *The Good Health* series. Co-author of *Blueprints Health Education* and a contributor to *The Primary Head* edited by Peter Mortimer, he is a core member of the National Primary Centre, having recently devised their award for Good Primary Practice.

Norman Scott

Norman Scott is the Health Education Co-ordinator for the LEA of a Metropolitan Borough in the North West. Formerly a deputy head teacher of a primary school, he has written guidance on Health Education, Sex Education and Pastoral

Responses to Drug Related Incidents emphasising whole school approaches to personal, social and health education. Having contributed to a number of national conferences, he is currently Chair of the North West Group of Health and Drug Education Co-ordinators and a member of RoSPA's National Safety Education Working Group.

Muriel Phillingham

Muriel Phillingham was formerly General Inspector for Personal, Social and Health Education for Lincolnshire, contributing to the LEA's National Curriculum support materials for Health Education. Author of several articles, *The Best From Events*, a booklet to support the use of special events in health education, and *Can We Find Out About Textiles*, she was previously a member of SEAC's Home Economics Committee, RoSPA's National Safety Committee and a member of NAIEA/NAEIAC National Executive as Regional Representative until 1993.

Ron Turner

Ron Turner is currently the Purchasing Manager for Acute Services at South Birmingham District Health Authority, having previously been the Commissioner for Health Promotion. A very experienced teacher and innovative health educator, he came to Birmingham as Schools Health Education Adviser, a post jointly funded by the LEA and District Health Authority, becoming the manager of the District Health Promotion Department. He has contributed to the development of health education at a local, regional and national level.

Diana Veasey

Diana Veasey is Research Fellow to the Marriage and Family Project in the department of Humanities and Religious Studies at Cheltenham and Gloucester College of Higher Education. She is working with teachers and others to produce resources for primary and secondary pupils and their teachers, which enable a journey of exploration towards a deeper understanding of relationships involved in marriage, sex, family and being single. She was formerly an Advisory Teacher for PSE.

David Wright

David Wright has been a primary school teacher in Birmingham for thirty years. Previously a deputy head teacher, he has recently co-ordinated The National Primary Centre and Birmingham LEA Project on The Management of Children's Behavioural and Emotional Needs. The project has produced two teacher packs, *Practice to Share*, and *Practice to Share 2*, both published by the National Primary Centre. They illustrate a range of effective school and classroom strategies for behaviour management in primary school.

CHAPTER 1

Health-Promoting Primary Schools: a Settings Context

John Lloyd

Introduction

In the last twenty years schools have become much more aware of the need to reconsider their role in their communities and in society at large, and the way in which they prepare children for the future and for adult life. The potential for schools to influence children's lifestyles has long been recognised.

As long ago as 1977, in the wake of the Committee on Child Health Services Report (Court 1977), the Department for Education and Science (DES 1977) issued guidance for schools which recommended that the prevention of ill health rather than its treatment was of concern for schools. It proposed that schools should be seen as crucially important in this work, if other agencies were to be successful. Further advice in 1986 (DES 1986) gave guidance on the curriculum, recommending a co-ordinated approach in schools. National Curriculum Council Curriculum Guidance (NCC 1990), for the first time not only clarified and defined health education, contexts and the whole school approach, but also offered a progression through its contributory components appropriate for pupils at each Key Stage of development.

Health education has in many primary schools become part of the everyday experience for pupils. It is an essential component of teaching and learning, either through the discrete subjects of the National Curriculum established by the Education Reform Act (ERA 1988) or through specific topics focusing on particular issues. In many respects it has become part of pupils' entitlement within the whole curriculum, as defined by the National Curriculum Council (NCC 1990a).

It has long been recognised that health education should begin in the home where, as HMI maintains,

patterns of behaviour and attitudes influence health for good or ill throughout life and will be well established before the child is five. (DES 1986)

Schools are required to promote attitudes, practices and understanding conducive to good health. However, it has become increasingly apparent that unless the curriculum provision is part of a coherent and planned programme; where teaching and learning about health education pervade throughout the school and are not restricted to the classroom; where the values promoted through such provision are not contradicted by the subtle messages received by children from the school environment, the 'hidden curriculum' and the daily life of the school; then health education is likely to be less effective than it should be in the promotion and development of self-esteem, well-being and ultimately healthy lifestyles.   As Trefor Williams notes,

> If what is learned in the classroom is not seen to be supported in practice by the school environment it will have little validity in the eyes of the students. Such teaching and learning will also need to demonstrate the validity of the principle to the lives of people in the wider community if it is to hold credence as an important and relevant area of human concern. (Williams 1985)

In perceiving that health education is not only about the curriculum but also about the acquired ability to make healthy choices, establish healthy patterns of behaviour and contribute, as Guidance 5 suggests, to the development of a healthy population, then the notion of the school as a 'health-promoting' institution becomes an irreducible concept. A concept which Lloyd and Morton (1992) argue,

> should not only recognise the school environment, the curriculum, teaching and learning strategies, but also take account of and acknowledge the role of the family, the community, and the role of health professionals who come into contact with children in the school.

However, there are those who argue that health education places too much emphasis on the individual to change behaviour rather than on collective and social action. Such action is seen as necessary to change environments and social conditions, and to challenge the political and economic inequalities which shape our lives and health choices. Successive reviews of health in Britain (Townsend and Davidson 1982, Whitehead 1988) have demonstrated marked differences in the distribution of disease and ill health by social class, race and gender. It is to the differences between health education and health promotion we now turn.

Health Education as the Basis for Health Promotion

The World Health Organisation (WHO 1969,1984) has defined health promotion as the process of educating people about health issues in order to enable them to increase control over, and improve, their health. This is seen in the context of people's everyday lives rather than focusing on people at risk from specific diseases.

It is clear that many external factors may affect individuals and communities and influence their health status. Factors such as the general environment, housing, employment and unemployment, income, and availability of and access to health care will all impact upon the individual and his or her well-being. For some, health education is perceived as too narrow a concept. They argue that besides promoting positive health behaviours, public health policy should adopt appropriate strategies which will restrict and thus prevent those health behaviours which are deemed to be unhealthy.

Such strategies seek to produce environmental and legislative changes in order to create a healthy society. However, such restriction may also arguably involve coercion, which is as ideologically unhealthy as those political, social and economic factors which help to cause ill health. It is perhaps not surprising that Young and Whitehead (1993) suggest that a dichotomy has arisen between those health educators,

> who focused on lifestyle risk factors, stressing the role of free choice in the adoption of a healthier lifestyle and those who focused on social and environmental changes and restriction on choices and personal lifestyle.

Without doubt the two strands are inextricably linked and as Young and Whitehead maintain, the extent to which individuals are in reality able to choose their lifestyles within the social and economic constraints which currently exist is questionable.

Tones (1989, 1990, 1993) and Lloyd (1991), however, argue convincingly that restrictions to choice are inappropriate and are about doing things to or for people, rather than enhancing their personal skills.

> The skills necessary to tackle the barriers which impede free choice and seek to empower people so that...the healthy choice becomes the easy choice (though definitely not the only choice!). (Tones 1990)

This process must begin in the primary school if it is to be effective in adult life.

Health education may therefore be seen as at the heart of health promotion, for as Ewles and Simnett (1991) propose,

> Without education for health, knowledge and understanding, there can be no informed decisions and actions to promote health.

Knowledge and understanding of what makes people healthy and unhealthy, attitudes and values clarification, and the development of skills in order to motivate people and enhance their decision-making are central to the educational model and to Anderson's (1986) concept of empowerment. But as Tones (1990) reflects,

> Even empowered individuals will find healthy choices difficult to make in circumstances which are not conducive to health.

This is true for schools if their own environments are not health-promoting. Tones further points out that despite this,

> Health education has an important and radical part to play by alerting people to the socio-economic and environmental threats to health and by creating professional and

public pressure for change...Health education is, therefore, not synonymous with health promotion but an essential ingredient, playing its part both in developing a healthy society and providing people with various competences and dispositions they need to take full advantage of it.

Health-promoting primary schools can be pivotal in this process.

Unfortunately, the *Health of the Nation* (DOH 1992), and the five key areas for action: coronary heart disease and stroke; cancers; mental illness; accidents and HIV and sexual health, described in each of the Key Area Handbooks (1993), seem to have little in common with the WHO commitment to being 'less concerned with preventing specific diseases and more concerned with promoting healthy lifestyles and feelings of well-being'. The targets set in *Health of the Nation* are in many respects 'victim blaming', even though health alliances between health services and schools are seen as playing a vital part in promoting good health. As French and Milner (1993) and Brown and Piper (1993) agree,

> The strategy has little to say about health as a state of positive well-being, and for the most part simply focuses itself (and us) on reducing the prevalence of disease in society. It is acutely individualistic in philosophy reflecting the dominant doctrine of personal responsibility. It unjustly ignores the overwhelming evidence of how structural issues influence health status.

In short, if you are poor, unemployed, live in inadequate housing and suffer ill health – it's your own fault! Moreover, what if your school is located in such an environment? As such, *Health of the Nation* blatantly ignores the evidence of inequalities.

Clearly, in order to become health-promoting, those engaged in health education in primary schools have to take account of these complexities in order that a 'settings approach' can be effectively implemented. Knowledge and understanding, information and informed choice will have to be balanced by a realistic and meaningful dialogue about the constraints.

The School Setting

Despite the narrow, individualistic and disease-specific philosophy behind them, all schools should reflect on the part that they can play in promoting health for the individual and the communities in which they exist, and on the important role they can have in achieving the *Health of the Nation* targets (DOH 1991). Schools are quite possibly one of the few settings where a fundamental goal of education, namely self-empowerment, can be related to health and to the provision of those skills and qualities necessary for achieving good health. After all, the children of today will be the adults of the year 2000, the conceptual date for the achievement of the *Health For All* campaign (WHO 1985).

The World Health Organisation's 'settings' approach to health recommends that health promotion should not be 'problem or disease' orientated, but should recognise that different populations in different settings will have different needs. These needs will require appropriate interventions and will necessarily take account of problems and disease, but will also recognise the relationships which exist between health and the environment and lifestyles – both are dependent on economic, social and political factors. These relationships in turn will impact upon the level of empowerment that populations in their respective settings will have.

Health-promoting settings may include at a macro level, as Baric (1992) suggests, Regional Health Authorities, District Health Authorities, Family Health Service Authorities, Community Services and Hospitals. These may well be part of a broader notion of the Health-Promoting Community setting which has the concept of the Healthy City (WHO 1990) at its heart. Intended to create alliances between institutions and organisations as well as the population, in theory (though not always in practice) the concept is about the development of public health policy based on broad understanding rather than narrow, medically defined health. Alliances between health services, local authorities, education, industry and commerce are all perceived as important contributors to Healthy Cities but each can be a setting in its own right. However, Baric (1992) rightly comments.

> Each setting is part of, and interdependent with, other parts of the system in terms of providing services or interventions in health.

The health-promoting school as a setting was first proposed in 1988 as a Resolution of the European Community Council of Ministers of Education. This resolution recognised not only the importance and value of health education in member states, but also the need for authorities,

> to make appropriate arrangements for co-ordinating health promoting measures between schools, families, health institutions and services, and the community, so that health education can be seen by children as a practical and not only theoretical part of their lives. (EC 1989)

Primary schools throughout the United Kingdom are required to consider health education as part of the formal curriculum, and as something which permeates the ethos of the school. *Guidance* for England and Wales (NCC 1990) emphasises that it should include,

> the quality of relationships within school, the example set by teachers, the physical environment and a school's facilities...and emphasising the importance of making use of opportunities to reinforce health education messages which occur throughout the daily life of a school.

Schools should be perceived as complex social institutions in which health promotion is not just aimed at pupils' health or school curriculum development, but which centres around the whole school environment and all aspects of school life. In order to achieve the European Resolution and the World Health Organisation recommendations (WHO 1991), the government has proposed that a pilot network of health-promoting schools should be established in order to,

> develop and assess the effectiveness of strategies for changing and shaping pupils' patterns of behaviour with the aim of safeguarding their long term health. (DOH 1991)

In regarding the setting up of the European Network of Health-Promoting Schools (HEA 1993) as an opportunity to study effective ways in which schools can contribute to the health of pupils, teachers and the wider community, the pilot project has identified a number of criteria based upon 'optimal' aims for schools as recommended by the World Health Organisation (WHO 1991).

These criteria for a health-promoting school are:
- commitment to the enhancement of the physical, social and psychological environment of the school;
- the manner in which it promotes the self-esteem of all pupils;
- good staff/pupil and pupil/pupil relationships;
- positive and productive school/family/community links;
- a stimulating and well balanced health education curriculum;
- the manner in which adults present themselves as role models to pupils;
- the employment of specialist community services for advice and support in health matters;
- the use of school health services beyond routine screening towards active involvement in the health education curriculum;
- how the school promotes the health of its staff;
- a wide range of stimulating and challenging mental, social, physical, and spiritual activities;
- the support and commitment of senior management to the concept of the school as a health-promoting institution.

However, in order for schools to achieve the status of 'health-promoting' not only is a commitment from the senior management desirable and necessary, but so also is the recognition by all concerned, including school governors, teachers, adults other than teachers who work in the school, parents and the children themselves, that they have a responsibility to ensure that the 'school setting' for health is effective.

The challenge is – how might we start this daunting process?

Key Features and Approaches

If being healthy is more than 'the absence of physical or mental disease' and is taken to include not only the physical aspects but also the psychological, emotional and spiritual needs of people, then self-esteem and well-being must be seen to be at the heart of the process.

Figure 1.1 illustrates this clearly, showing that primary schools (and indeed secondary schools), in order to become health-promoting, need to develop action around the principal features which are interrelated both within and between each of the inner and outer segments of the model. The commitment to becoming health-promoting should be clearly stated in the school aims and apparent in the school development plan, recognising the need for appropriate resource allocation. In this respect the role of the governing body is of paramount importance.

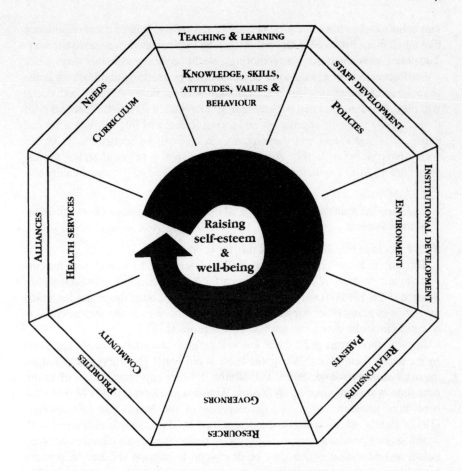

Figure 1.1 Key Features of the Health-Promoting School

Institutional development refers to the management of the school, its ethos and its values, and to what Nias, Southworth and Yeomans (1988) call 'the culture of collaboration'. At the heart of this culture, respect, empathy and genuineness is accorded to all staff and children; people are valued as individuals; mutual dependency is fostered and encouraged; people are open and honest in their dealings with each other and a secure and less stressful atmosphere is engendered. The need for a physical environment conducive to institutional development of this sort cannot be understated!

Such a culture will also be fostered through staff development. Staff development for teachers and for non-teaching staff is vital, and may well involve a broad range of providers. Staff development will almost certainly relate to the review and development of policies on key issues such as pastoral care, equal opportunity, sex education, behaviour and discipline, child protection and bullying, and health and safety. Successful policies are those which engage everyone in the process and allow individuals and groups to reflect on their own learning and beliefs and to have some ownership of the policy. It is of great importance that all staff are involved if any policy is to be implemented in a consistent way. The policy to become 'health-promoting' should be managed in this way.

Staff development must also be contextualised by teaching and learning in the school and by the recognition that health knowledge, skills, attitudes and values will play a fundamental part in determining behaviour at all levels. Teachers need to use a wide range of approaches and styles, formal and informal, didactic and experiential, individual and participatory, in order to be successful. What are their strengths, what do they still need to develop at a personal and/or professional level? As O'Donnell and Taylor (1990) remark in relation to 'healthy colleges',

> Promoting the health and well-being of all members of the college means promoting effective learning.

Surely this is as true for schools as it is for colleges?

The answer to such questions may well be determined by reference to the curriculum and to the statutory requirements for health education provision within Science (DES 1991). It may also take account of those other opportunities which may arise in many other subjects of the curriculum, or from the implementation of cross-curricular themes and whole school projects.

In curriculum terms pupil needs are well defined. But what of needs identified by the pupils themselves? We ignore these at our peril! The importance of starting with children's experience and valuing it as an important aspect of health education was recognised by Williams, Wetton and Moon (HEA 1989) in their innovative research and in the development of the *Health for Life* resource (1989). Pupils' needs will also be determined by those people concerned with health service provision, emphasising the importance of those alliances between health and education which may be developed to support children in primary schools and in their communities.

If it is the community setting for health which will determine the priorities to which alliances will respond, then it is the governors and school staff who will determine priorities for the primary school and the resources allocation. This will include a consideration of issues such as staffing, teaching resources, availability of time and improvement of the physical environment of the school.

Parents have a major contribution to make to the development of healthy schools, as partners and contributors to the curriculum and certainly not simply as helpers, or, as Braun and Combes (1987) express concern about, 'passive receivers of information'. Nor should parents be seen as an alternative source for school funds in these days of depleted school income, capped LEA budgets and almost arbitrary levels of Standard Spending Assessments. Shouldn't a health-promoting school be empowering parents to challenge such inequalities of funding anyway?

A positive relationship with parents, then, is a vital part of the health-promoting process and a significant factor in the school's institutional development.

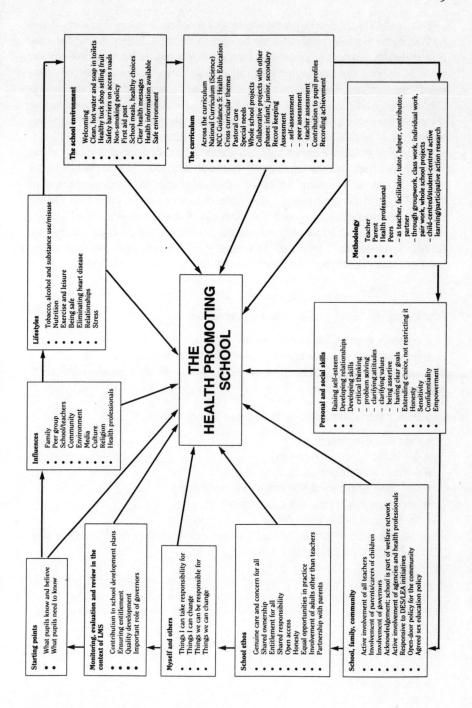

The school environment

- Welcoming
- Clean, hot water and soap in toilets
- Healthy tuck shop selling fruit
- Safety barriers on access roads
- Non-smoking policy
- First aid post
- School meals, healthy choices
- Clear health messages
- Health information available
- Safe environment

The curriculum

- Across the curriculum
- National Curriculum (Science)
- NCC Guidance 5: Health Education
- Cross curricular themes
- Pastoral care
- Special needs
- Whole school projects
- Collaborative projects with other phases: infant, junior, secondary
- Record keeping
- Assessment
  - self-assessment
  - peer assessment
  - teacher assessment
- Contribution to pupil profiles
- Recording achievement

Methodology

- Teacher
- Parent
- Health professional
- Peers
  - as teacher, facilitator, tutor, helper, contributor, partner
  - through groupwork, class work, individual work, pair work, whole school projects
  - child-centred/student-centred active learning/participative action research

Lifestyles

- Tobacco, alcohol and substance use/misuse
- Nutrition
- Exercise and leisure
- Being safe
- Eliminating heart disease
- Relationships
- Stress

Influences

- Family
- Peer group
- School/teachers
- Community
- Environment
- Media
- Culture
- Religion
- Health professionals

THE HEALTH PROMOTING SCHOOL

Personal and social skills

- Raising self-esteem
- Developing relationships
- Developing skills
  - critical thinking
  - problem solving
  - clarifying attitudes
  - clarifying values
  - being assertive
  - having clear goals
- Extending choice, not restricting it
- Honesty
- Sensitivity
- Confidentiality
- Empowerment

Starting points

- What pupils know and believe
- What pupils need to know

Monitoring, evaluation and review in the context of LMS

- Contribution to school development plans
- Ensuring entitlement
- Quality development
- Important role of governors

Myself and others

- Things I can take responsibility for
- Things I can change
- Things we can be responsible for
- Things we can change

School ethos

- Genuine care and concern for all
- Shared ownership
- Entitlement for all
- Shared responsibility
- Open access
- Honesty
- Equal opportunities in practice
- Involvement of adults other than teachers
- Partnership with parents

School, family, community

- Active involvement of all teachers
- Involvement of parents/carers of children
- Involvement of governors
- Acknowledgement; school is part of welfare network
- Active involvement of agencies and health professionals
- Responsive to DES/LEA initiatives
- Open-door policy for the community
- Agreed sex education policy

Figure 1.2 The Health-Promoting School

This model for the health-promoting school was first developed in some detail by Lloyd and Morton (1992). As can be seen in Figure 1.2, they define the concept of health-promoting under key issues for schools, recognising the importance of appropriate starting points; influences; lifestyles; the school environment; curriculum; methodology; personal and social skills; family and community; school ethos; what can be changed; and monitoring, evaluation and review in the context of the local management of schools. To this list, of course, we must now add the requirements of school inspection.

It is a cyclical model which not only recognises the relationship that each box has with the next, but also the relationship that each has with the other boxes in the model. The model has some utilitarian advantages over the model described in Figure 1.1, in that it can be used to pose questions about health education and the promotion of health in the school. Each box can be used to audit a school's existing practice in order to identify omissions, celebrate good practice and initiate further development (Lloyd and Morton 1992b). For example, here are some audit questions developed from the boxes by primary school teachers.

Starting Points

In planning the health curriculum does our school:

- consider what pupils already know and believe?
- reflect on what pupils need to know relative to their age?

Influences

In planning the health curriculum does our school consider:

- the family context?
- the influence of peer groups?
- the role models presented by teachers?
- the effect of the local and school environments?
- the cultural norms of the community?
- the religion/faiths of the pupils?
- the provision of health care and access to the support from health professionals in our community?

Lifestyles

Do we plan for lifestyle issues adequately and as part of a whole school approach to:

- tobacco, alcohol and substance use?
- nutrition and diet?
- exercise and leisure?
- being safe?
- developing relationships?
- reducing stress?

Environment

Does our school recognise the importance of the quality of the environment?
- Is our school welcoming to visitors?
- Is the school clean, and is hot water and soap available in the toilets?
- Does our tuck shop provide healthy alternatives such as fruit?
- Do we have safety barriers at the access points to the school?
- Is the school's smoking policy effectively implemented?
- Are any of our school staff qualified in Emergency Aid?
- Do our school meals provide healthy food choices?
- Does our school display consistent health messages throughout?
- Do we provide health information for pupils, teachers, parents and visitors?
- Do we provide a safe environment for our pupils?

Similar questions can be asked for each heading in the model. If the answer to any of these is 'no' then clearly action needs to be taken to bring about change. The danger of any audit is that it 'looks busy' but can become an end in itself. In order to bring about change, to make it happen, we need to keep asking ourselves:

- What can I take responsibility for?
- What things can I change?
- What things can we be responsible for?
- What things can we change?

Through such questioning the skills of critical thinking, problem-solving, attitude and value clarification, decision-making and goal-setting will be enacted. In so doing, all participants will be empowered to play their part in raising self-esteem and developing a sense of well-being, which will contribute collectively to the good health of the school.

Conclusions

In defining health in these terms, the purpose of the book is to focus on the key issues, from the early years to transition to secondary schooling, that every primary school will face in becoming a health-promoting setting.

The roles of those working in the health service, governors and parents are explored in some detail. Policies relating to lifestyle issues, sexual health, child protection and children's behaviour, all extremely relevant and current, are considered carefully. The curriculum context, whole school development, and monitoring, evaluation and inspection issues are raised and in carrying the debate forward, the question 'How can schools move from the rhetoric to the realities of school life?' is posed.

Finally, implications for teaching and learning are reflected upon in what for many is not only a curriculum entitlement for all but also an extremely sensitive and often controversial part of primary school life.

At the end of the day, perhaps we have to temper what is possible with a degree of pragmatism and accept that there is a place for media campaigns and restrictions on some activities (few health educators would disagree with the argument that tobacco advertising should be banned!) and that public health policy, *Healthy Cities* and the like can contribute to a healthy population. In so doing, however, schools must reflect on the purpose of education, which is about extending choices, not restricting them; empowerment not coercion; self-esteem and well-being and not illness and disease. As Tones (1990) succinctly states,

> Without education there will be no challenge to unhealthy social structures and practices...there is nothing new in the assertion that education is at heart radical and subversive – or it ought to be!

The health-promoting primary school should be seeking to move forward on all fronts at all times; it should be as challenging for those in the organisation as for those outside it.

CHAPTER 2

Purchasing Practical Health Promotion for the Primary School: a District Health Authority Perspective

Ron Turner

Introduction

If primary schools are to become more health-promoting in both their practice and ethos, then it is important that they actively seek information about, and gain access to and support from, an appropriate range of District Health Authority (DHA) services.

DHAs must also be pro-active in making links with the primary schools within their boundaries, if they are serious about improving both the present and future health status of the children they serve.

This chapter, therefore, is aimed at enabling primary schools to understand the ways in which DHAs contract for health promotion services, what those services are, and how to make contact with them.

Similarly, it encourages DHAs to purchase health promotion services which seek to understand the practical day-to-day realities of life in primary schools, and as a consequence develop with Local Education Authority advisers, teachers, pupils and parents locally targeted and 'bespoke' health promotion programmes. These should be aimed at achieving step by step improvements in the development of school health promotion planning and policies, in the health status of the pupils, and in the development of the relationships between the professionals and the communities involved.

Changes in the National Health Service

The National Health Service (NHS) has undergone enormous changes and upheaval in the last five years. Perhaps the most far-reaching changes can be attributed to the White Paper *Working for Patients* which came into effect in April 1991.

Fig. 1

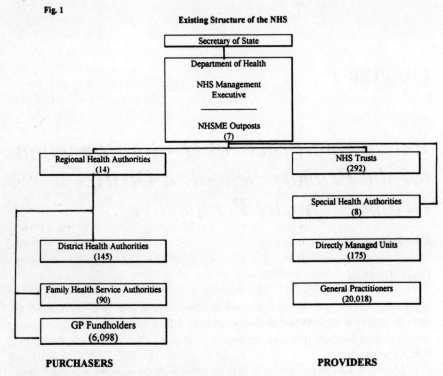

Existing Structure of the NHS

Secretary of State

Department of Health

NHS Management Executive

NHSME Outposts (7)

Regional Health Authorities (14)

NHS Trusts (292)

Special Health Authorities (8)

District Health Authorities (145)

Directly Managed Units (175)

Family Health Service Authorities (90)

General Practitioners (20,018)

GP Fundholders (6,098)

PURCHASERS   PROVIDERS

Figure 2.1 Existing Structure of the NHS

This White Paper was aimed at creating an 'internal' market within the NHS. In simple terms it changed the service from being directly managed into one where services are bought and contracted for. Known colloquially as the Purchaser-Provider split, since 1991 this reform has developed apace, with the establishment of Trusts and GP fund holding.

At District level the system works as follows:
DHAs now receive a sum of money based loosely on the population of the district (although there are subsequent additions for such things as teaching hospitals, mortality rates etc). With this money they commission a range of services to meet the health needs of the population for which they are responsible. The role of the Director of Public Health and his or her colleagues, one of whom is usually a health promotion specialist, is to undertake this on-going assessment, and therefore to help to shape the Health Authority's purchasing strategy.

Purchasing

On an annual basis the DHA produces a Purchasing Plan in which it outlines the range of health services which it will be buying for the following year. This plan is produced in October/November and goes out for formal public consultation.

The plan indicates where the DHA's financial resources will be placed in the following year, e.g. how much money will be spent on Acute Care (procedures such as surgery in District General Hospitals) and Primary Care (services that are provided in the community). It will also prioritise resources for certain target groups such as elderly people over 70 years of age, ethnic minorities and people at greater risk from certain diseases. The plan can also signal a shift in resources from one sector of the NHS to another.

Strategically the Department of Health is aiming to shift services out of the Acute sector into the Primary sector, mainly because it envisages that this will save money. However, market research shows that most people would prefer to be treated in their own communities, and not have to travel and spend time overnight in hospitals.

Another reason for this shift of emphasis is because of the government's belief that people and communities should start to take more responsibility for their own health, and that the public health agenda should not be entirely controlled by the medical profession.

These are huge issues for debate which probably belong elsewhere. They do, however, impinge on society at every level, and they are certainly instrumental in shaping a DHA's concept and vision of health promotion.

Contracting

Once a DHA has established which services it will purchase, it will begin to negotiate with a range of organisations regarding contracts.

Basically, a contract is an agreement to exchange a sum of money in return for a service delivered at a negotiated level of activity and quality.

For example, a DHA might decide it wants to buy 10 eye cataract operations at £1500 per operation. The quality indicator might be that patients wait no longer than 13 weeks for this procedure, and that no more than one patient will have to return for further treatment within 12 months due to infection or complications. This is a simple, hypothetical example from the Acute sector. However, it does illustrate how complicated and labyrinthine the setting and monitoring of contracts can become.

The above example also applies to a procedure which is reasonably easy to isolate and measure. To a certain extent the problem and the solution are already known. The effectiveness of the procedure or intervention (the operation) can therefore be measured.

Issues become much more complicated and uncertain when we move out of curative medicine into the field of prevention and health promotion. Important questions in this area are:

● What is it that we are trying to measure?
● Over what period of time are we measuring it?
● To what factors can success be attributable?
● What is meant by 'effectiveness' in the field of health promotion?
● Who will carry out the health promotion?

A DHA therefore has to develop a service specification for health promotion which not only describes the range of services required, but goes some way towards answering some of the above questions. To some extent, the *Health of the Nation* White Paper has helped to inform this process.

Health of the Nation

The government has recognised the need for a National Health Promotion Strategy, and the *Health of the Nation* document is effectively its first attempt at this.

The main aim behind the Health of the Nation is simple - to improve the health of people living in England.

In order to do this, the government says we must

Focus on promoting good health, and preventing disease as much as on care and treatment.

(DOH, 1992)

Health of the Nation identifies five key areas in which the above activity should take place. They are:

– Coronary Heart Disease
– Cancers
– Mental Health
– Accidents
– Sexual Health (including HIV/AIDS)

For some of these areas the government has set a series of targets to be achieved by the years 2000–2005.

Healthy Alliances

Health of the Nation recognises that the promotion of health cannot be achieved by the NHS alone. Indeed it is imperative that DHAs and Trusts influence and work together with other statutory and voluntary agencies, in order to develop effective health promotion programmes.

Although the reforms have encouraged DHAs to become 'champions of the people's' health, *Health of the Nation* recognises that they must do this in a variety of ways, not least through facilitating a contribution from a range of other private and public organisations.

Health of the Nation has been extremely influential in shaping a local DHA's Health Promotion Strategy. However, it is interesting to note that the vision of health promotion outlined in *Health of the Nation* is still very much a traditional or medical one, based on the assumptions that the causes of ill health are to be found in unhealthy lifestyles, and that if individuals can be educated, empowered, or even coerced into adopting healthier lifestyles then the population's health will improve. *Health of the Nation* says little about inequalities in health which result from social class, ethnicity and the environment.

Models of Health Promotion

Without becoming immersed in the theoretical debate taking place in health promotion circles, it is both relevant and important for schools to understand the philosophy informing the practice of NHS health promotion professionals with whom they may be working. It is fair to say, too, that one professional's health promotion style and practice can be extremely different from another's, depending on each person's training, professional culture and experience.

It is therefore important that the DHA, in purchasing these professional health promotion services, is itself guided by a Health Promotion Strategy which is based on a set of agreed values and beliefs with regard to both health promotion theory and practice.

For example, if one of the objectives of the DHA, set out in its Purchasing Plan, is to reduce smoking prevalence among 11-15 year olds by 33 per cent in nine months (a *Health of the Nation* target) then it has to purchase a health promotion programme that can achieve this.

As already mentioned, NHS staff alone cannot achieve this objective, so a DHA may contract with a specialist Health Promotion Provider department to provide teacher training in collaboration with a Local Education Authority (LEA) on, say, smoking education in the classroom. The training programme would probably be aimed at primary school staff/parents on the assumption that the subsequent education the pupils received from their teacher would act as a preventative or prophylactic measure, i.e. it would stop or delay them from starting smoking. This practice is based on the reasonable assumption that it is easier to stop primary school pupils from starting the habit (they are younger and more positive in their reaction to adults' messages), than it is to encourage secondary age pupils to give up (during adolescence they are much more receptive to peer group pressure, and are 'naturally' rebellious).

It may be true that the targeting of the primary school will be more effective in the long run, but this may not achieve the DHA's rather ambitious nine-month objective. It follows that the DHA will wish to purchase other health promotion activities that are effective in the short term and that go some way towards achieving its annual objectives, without losing sight of what can be beneficial in terms of health improvement in the long term.

Therefore a DHA will purchase a range of activities from a range of different agencies in order to try to reduce the prevalence of smoking in teenagers. This might include activities such as public health doctors putting pressure on a local authority's environmental services department, a crack-down on retailers selling cigarettes to under-16s, and an on-going joint-education programme for teachers (as outlined above).

A DHA's broad approach to health promotion can be illustrated by the following simple model based on Tannahill (1994).

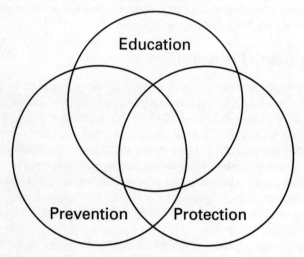

Figure 2.2 Tannahill's Model of Health Promotion

Health-promotion activities are wider, therefore, than the provision of education programmes, and a DHA will purchase activities in the area of prevention and protection to complement them. The following diagram helps to explain this further.

Disease Prevention	Health Education	Health Protection
e.g. Child Immunisation	e.g. Teacher Training Resources & Information Services	e.g. Seat Belt Legislation No Smoking Areas in Public Place

Figure 2.3 Health Promotion Activities

The Health-Promoting School

Research has shown that many adult health problems start in infancy and childhood (for example, five-year-olds in a recent USA study were shown to have raised cholesterol levels as a result of their diet). Therefore DHAs are interested in developing health promotion programmes which are aimed at young people. Such programmes are seen as efficient ways of reducing the development of risk factors for disease, (e.g. reducing raised cholesterol as a risk factor for coronary heart disease and stroke) and of developing positive attitudes, skills, and health-related behaviour.

However, with reference to the health promotion model described above, it has become apparent to DHAs that activities such as information-giving and discussion about health issues that may form part of classroom practice, (as part of a health education curriculum) are not considered enough, in themselves, to be lastingly effective.

Recent thinking says that in order for health education messages to lead to sustainable knowledge and behaviour change, they must be reinforced in a whole school context.

Understanding gained in the classroom can either be reinforced and supported or completely undermined by what happens outside the classroom.

(Smith *et al*,1993)

It is therefore extremely important that the messages about health given by a school to its pupils and parents are seen to be consistent across the 'wider curriculum' including the classroom, the school environment, and links with the family and community.

If these messages and practices are not consistent, then 'a hidden curriculum' develops, through which pupils can perceive the school as manipulative and less than honest in its approach to health education. Examples of non-health-promoting practice abound, but two are of particular concern to District Health Authorities. First, the practice of classroom teaching about healthy diet, yet not addressing the nutritional content of school canteen food, or the diet that pupils consume at home. Secondly, the issue of smoking education in schools where pupils see teachers smoking in the staff room, or where pupils go home to live with parents who smoke.

In order to fulfil its commitment, declared in *Health of the Nation*, to champion the health of the local population, DHAs are eager to work with Local Education Authorities and individual schools in order to progress the development of a more health-promoting ethos. Such an ethos would include:

• The development and context of the health education curriculum;
• The implementation of health-related policies (e.g. in relation to smoking and diet);
• The planned involvement of outside agencies and other professionals;
• The further development in teachers and parents of the concept of a health-promoting primary school.

However, in their eagerness to develop healthy alliances with the education sector, DHAs must be wary of falling into the trap of defining health only in terms of physical health. Such definition would be conducive to maintaining the *status quo* with regard to the ownership of health issues by the medical profession. Health also has social, mental, emotional and spiritual dimensions.

Health is far from an objective concept, and all schools need to play an important role in supporting their pupils and communities in developing their own individual concepts of health. Part of that should be about empowering pupils and parents to offer constructive criticism of received medical opinion and hierarchy.

Let's look in more detail at the services and support which primary schools can expect from local NHS providers. It should be noted that these local services are being purchased by the DHA in order to ensure that collaboration between Health and Education staff results in the overall achievement of better health for the pupils and parents living within the DHA's boundaries.

The District Health Promotion Department

Progressive DHAs will ensure that health promotion in schools remains broadly creative, and will encourage its development by purchasing health promotion specialists to work alongside LEA staff and teachers.

Health promotion specialists (often called Health Promotion Officers or Advisers) are managed within Health Promotion Departments and come from a variety of backgrounds. Specialists who work on school or young people's programmes ought to have previous experience in teaching, lecturing or youth work.

A recent study in Welsh schools (Smith *et al.*, Health Promotion Wales, 1989-

Agencies/professionals involved in schools' health promotion, Wales 1989/90		
Agency/Professional	Schools using agency/professional %	Agency/Professional felt to be most helpful* %
District health education/ promotion unit	86	49
LEA advisory teachers	77	43
HPAW	63	7
TACADE	62	6
School nurse	53	14
Health visitor	51	12
Family planning	39	5
Local drugs service	37	6
Local AIDS co-ordinators	29	3
General Practitioner	22	0
School medical officer	8	0
Dentist	25	1
Police	16	5
Automobile Association	7	0
Other	49	9
Number of schools (–100%)	(87)	(87)

* Percentages do not add up to 100 as schools could name up to three 'most helpful' agencies/professionals if more than three were used.

Figure 2.4 Agencies/Professionals involved in Health Promotion in Wales

90) shows these professionals as being the most helpful with regard to resources, training and policy development – see Figure 2.4.

Health Promotion Departments are increasingly being seen as centres that support professional development for health workers. Figure 2.5 (after Fitzpatrick 1993) illustrates the scope of support provided to teachers by primary health care workers.

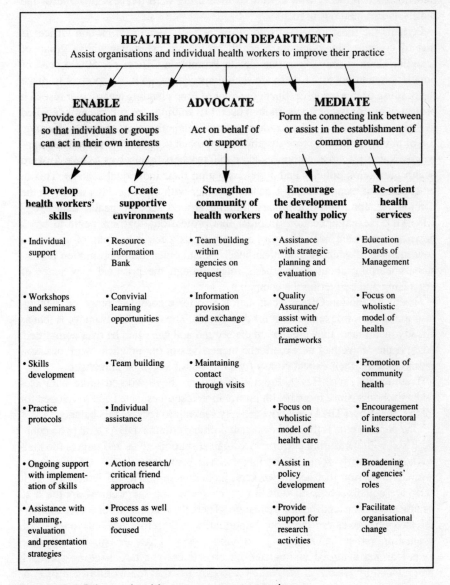

Figure 2.5 Primary health care support to teachers

In practical terms, Health Promotion Departments stock a wide range of resources for health and other professionals, including videos, teaching packs, leaflets and posters. More importantly, Health Promotion Officers can give teachers up to the minute advice on the quality of resources. Better resourced departments will have Health Promotion Officers whose remit is schools. They are committed to training teachers, parents and governors in health education and health promotion issues and skills. They are also looking for schools to partner pilot research projects with a view to measuring defectiveness in some of the materials and methods used.

Perhaps the most important role of the Schools Health Promotion Officer is that of co-ordinating/planning a health promotion campaign with a group of schools. There is only about one Health Promotion Officer per 50000 head of population, and not all of these are school specialists, so it is important to make the best use of this resource. Spending a lot of time planning a particular research project in one or two schools, though useful (if findings are subsequently applied to their future work), can be a rather esoteric, and perhaps not the most effective, use of public money. A more sustainable approach is to develop projects or campaigns which resource, enthuse, and enable teachers themselves to take forward health promotion policies and activities within their individual schools. This in practice could mean bringing teachers together with other health workers in the community, for multi-disciplinary training around specific health issues (e.g. HIV/AIDS sexual education) in order that professional barriers begin to break down. Also, it can mean planning a health focus week in a group of schools, a consequence of which would mean teachers and other health promotion professionals learning about each other's roles through the practical experience of organising and delivering the campaign.

Health Promotion Officers can therefore offer a complete range of training, resourcing policy developments for the schools. The main disadvantage is that as already mentioned, they are few on the ground and can often be over committed. Also, if they have had no experience themselves in the practical work of classroom teaching, their expectations of what is possible can be unrealistic.

Traditionally, too, Health Promotion Officers have worked more with secondary schools, since more health information resources have been developed for that sector. Wiser DHAs are now actively seeking to redress this balance.

One point to note is that in the present political climate, DHAs tend to be rather obsessed with measuring performance against set objectives and targets (no matter how arbitrarily some of the targets have been formulated). Consequently, teachers may find that health workers, including some Health Promotion Officers, are equally obsessed with a rather narrow and hierarchical approach to health promotion and health education. There is a belief abroad that teacher-selected objectives are the more important, and therefore the only ones worth evaluating, rather than accepting that pupil-selected goals are equally important, as is learning acquired without pre-set objectives. The target-setting approach propounded by *Health of the Nation* also assumes that the worth of a project or campaign can be determined only by the attainment of behavioural objectives, whereas it is well known that worthwhile learning is often personal, obscure, and private, and only some learning appears as behavioural change.

District HIV/AIDS Services

At the time of the 'AIDS Scare' in the late 1980s, the government gave Regional Health Authorities a considerable pot of money for HIV/AIDS research and Development. Many District Health Promotion Departments successfully bid for these monies in order to appoint specialist HIV/AIDS workers. Again, progressive departments saw the need to link HIV/AIDS into the broader sex education curriculum in schools and appointed at least one schools HIV/AIDS Officer who would have a background in developing this most sensitive area of the curriculum in schools.

However, other workers were appointed as a result of this funding who had little to do with schools or prevention and these workers were often managed in a separate unit within the District Health Authority.

Since the 1991 Purchaser-Provider split and subsequent reorganisations, some DHAs have provider HIV Departments which now contain specialists such as young people's sexual health workers. An enterprising primary school might consider accessing these resources too (if indeed they exist within a district) bearing in mind that difficulty of co-ordination is paramount when working with a multi-professional organisation such as the NHS. Again, health promotion specialists should be in the lead position to do this mediation for the school. Although in reality some primary schools can find themselves approached by a range of health professionals from a variety of departments, each of whom is not aware of the others' roles and intentions.

School Health Services

To a certain extent school health services have traditionally been responsible for the disease prevention element of the health promotion model outlined earlier. Schools will already be familiar with the service components, such as hearing and vision screening, immunisations and dental services, which are delivered by school nurses, doctors and dentists.

It is important to stress, however, that since the 1991 reforms and the introduction of the Children Act (1989) DHAs are beginning to commission a more comprehensive schools' health service, integrated within a district child health service. These services will usually be provided from within a Community Trust. They could also include systems for the assessment and management of children with emotional behavioural problems (including individual counselling on health issues), the management and educational implications of common health problems, and liaison with hospital services, primary health care teams, the NSPCC, police, and other community voluntary groups.

Good practice should ensure that schools have information in the form of a Directory of Services from the provider organisations (the Trusts).

As a result of the above, school nurses in particular wish to expand their role to encompass a health education input into schools. There are, therefore, enormous opportunities for primary schools to plan with nurses and other professionals in order to ensure that health issues are well integrated into the taught and informal curriculum. It is important, however, for the teaching staff to retain control of, and take responsibility for, delivering the education aspects of this health curriculum to pupils and parents. There are dangers in assuming that the health promotion input into the school is the sole responsibility of health professionals. The first danger is that it does not encourage collaboration and shared learning amongst the professionals involved. Secondly, the health agenda could be perceived as having a lower status by the pupils and parents if teachers are not seen to be actively involved in it. Thirdly, if health staff are brought in, even in a planned way, to table a series of health topics, it tends to be a didactic rather than heuristic model that is adopted, possibly a litany of do's and don'ts about a particular issue, the hidden message of which is saying to pupils that health, in essence, is owned by health service professionals.

Conclusions

Perhaps a challenge for District Health Authorities in the post-reform world is how best to ensure, through purchasing, that collaboration between different professional groups, does take place within the field of health promotion – collaboration that leads to effective health promotion being delivered and sustained within the primary school. Often, barriers to professional collaboration lie not between NHS staff and teachers, but amongst different groups of NHS professionals. It would seem that the District Health Promotion Department offers the best focus and opportunity for planned mediation and support amongst these different groups.

CHAPTER 3

The Role of Parents and Governors

Ron Morton

Schools and Parents – A Healthy Relationship?

In *A survey of health education policies in schools* (HEA 1993) it was stated that primary schools are more likely than secondary schools to have developed a policy on health education in response to active encouragement from parents and governors, particularly if those schools are located in predominantly middle-class areas. Perhaps somewhat paradoxically, the report went on to conclude that, generally speaking, parents and governors had not played a significant part in the decision to develop a policy. In conclusion the report stated:

> many schools have broadened their health education provision beyond the curriculum, recognising the value of a health promoting school...
> However, few schools have as yet recognised the need to involve non-teaching staff, parents and other adults who help in the school process.

This apparent problem was also highlighted in the 1994 national evaluation of TACADE's *Skills for the Primary School Child* (Lloyd 1994). It was discovered that the strategy least explored by schools seeking to address issues of self-esteem and personal safety was the parents' workshop material contained within the resource pack, which was aimed at schools developing skills and understanding in partnership with parents. Reasons given were primarily those of time and unfamiliarity with what was perceived as still fairly new material. Nevertheless, the fact remains that for many parents and schools, working together is less than symbiotic and more often much less than a partnership. Yet no other area of the curriculum appears to offer more scope for a coalescence of interests between schools and parents than that of health education and the promotion of health. This general lack of partnership seems to occur despite the fact that (during the last decade in particular) the notion of parents and schools as partners in children's education has been legislated for and actively promoted through a variety of initiatives. These include the 1981 Education Act, the 1993 Education

Act, the highly significant 1988 Education Reform Act and the 'Parents Charter' (1992) which states:'This charter will help you to become a more effective partner in your child's education.'

The involvement of parents in schools has never been as straightforward as legislation would have us believe, mainly because parents are not a homogeneous group and, even with the introduction of a nationally prescribed curriculum, neither are schools. Furthermore, the expectations parents have of schools and schools have of parents often have wide variations, arising from differing educational traditions. This results in perceptions of the roles of teachers and parents which are based on competing ideologies. These perceptions are held as much by parents as they are by teachers.

Despite the fact that parents are not homogeneous as a group, and arguably neither are teachers, school-based action research will usually show that parents generally perceive similar needs for their children in terms of health. Only in the area of sex education might this unified perception differ.

The notion of partnership between parents and teachers in promoting the health of children is clearly and simply defined by Braun and Combes (1987): 'We argue that a partnership must be based on a relationship which assumes equality between parent and teacher.'

Parental Involvement and the Need for Partnership

Mary Warnock, in her 1978 Report, states directly that the partnership between parents and professional should be:

'...a partnership, and ideally an equal one...we are well aware that professional help cannot be wholly effective, if at all so, unless it builds upon the parents' capacity to be involved. Thus we see the relationship as a dialogue between parents and helpers working in partnership...Parents can be effective partners only if professionals take notice of what they say and of how they express their needs and treat their contribution as intrinsically important.'

(para.9.6, p.151)

All schools come into contact with parents at some time, and communicate in a variety of ways. Effective communication to parents is of course important and to many schools this is considered to be the basis of a good relationship. However, communication is too often one way, from the school to the home, and this is a far cry from the notion of partnership, the basis of which is that both parents and teachers have equal status, and their contributions to the learning process are of equal importance. This idea could be judged as naïve, perhaps, if applied to areas of the curriculum other than health, where most parents might be excluded, at least by teachers, on the grounds of lacking specific expertise or knowledge.

This does not necessarily apply in the case of health education, where the knowledge and expertise of parents is often as good as that of teachers or can be accessed by determined parents as easily as it can for teachers (perhaps with the exception of sex education – see Chapter 5 by Diana Veasey). The incentive to do so can be greater for parents than for teachers. There is, therefore, a strong case to suggest that schools which fail to involve parents, or exclude them from the learning processes of health education, relegate themselves merely to teaching health education. Schools that work together with parents can more justifiably claim to be health-promoting schools – and there is a difference, especially if health education is not only informing children about what health choices they may be faced with, but also about the empowerment of children to act in their own interests. How is it possible to exclude parents, given that children,in order to exercise their empowerment and to be effective guardians of their own health, will need to support their parents? To exclude parents from the health education of their children, or even to subordinate their role, will undermine, perhaps totally negate, the empowerment that good health education and health promotion seeks to provide.

The effective primary school already has at least the foundations for the partnership involvement that health promotion requires and that, perhaps uniquely, the health curriculum can facilitate. At the present time, all schools, as a matter of good practice, are expected to have policies for parental involvement and will be judged on the degree of that involvement by OFSTED inspections. For instance: the OFSTED inspection will seek to determine, 'How effectively does the school involve parents in the education of their children and the life of their school?' Indeed, in the technical paper within the handbook there is a clear reference to partnership: 'In the best practice considerable attention is given to developing partnership between home and school.' This is presumably because it is recognised that through a partnership there are improved chances of teachers, parents and pupils sharing expectations and understanding, thereby enhancing the quality of teaching and learning, and resulting in the raising of educational standards and achievements.

Recent legislation has meant that schools are now accepting increased parental involvement both in the management of the school and in the classroom. Some schools embrace the opportunity and behave positively. They encourage a relationship that they believe will assist the development of the school in its set course and public accountability. Other schools, realising there is little choice but to conform at least to the basic expectations determined by legislation, still engage with parents at levels that fall short of partnership. Gordon (1969) refers to a five-point scale identifying the different roles parents might play and suggests the following: parents as supporters; parents as learners; parents as teachers of their own children; parents as teacher aides and volunteers in a classroom; parents as policy makers and partners.

With the introduction and implementation of the 1981 Act, Warnock emphasised the positive benefits of partnership, especially in the area of special educational needs. Anything less than a partnership is perceived by Wolfendale (1983) and others as: being in the role of 'client'; dependent on experts' opinions; passive – apparently in need of direction; peripheral to decision-making; in effect that of a subordinate. Wolfendale supports Warnock's statement on parental partnership by claiming that parents who are active and central to decision-making are perceived as having equal strengths and expertise and are able to contribute as well as to receive services. Repeatedly, the argument for parental partnership, especially in relation to children's health, is heard from researchers who are addressing the issues of health education from a variety of perspectives.

Like Gordon, Braun and Combes (1987), in their study of parental involvement in children's health, observe parental involvement in schools as operating along a continuum which begins with parents as receivers, as helpers, as contributors. Up to this point many teachers feel comfortable and in control. They take the lead in making suggestions, in setting the direction and (above all), in making decisions. The next step is that of partnership, where the role of parents and teachers is that of equals, the decision-making is shared, and suggestions to support the decision-making come from all concerned and have a common aim and focus. Teachers who stop short of partnership generally do so either because they feel threatened as professionals and find themselves in danger of losing the control element of their position, or because they cannot manage the diverse interest levels of parents which they see as over-riding that of the common interest. However, it is not unreasonable to expect that many parents, through their own experiences of relationships and interaction with others, would be sensitive to such a response from a teacher and therefore would manage the developing partnership until the perceived 'threat' has shown no substance.

Braun and Combes take the parental continuum beyond that of partnership and list a further category of parental involvement as 'parents who make decisions which over-ride schools'. This is extended into perhaps the ultimate level of parental involvement, where 'parents make decisions which the school complies with'. Both these levels are beyond the notion of 'a partnership of equals' and can arguably have a more comfortable and less contentious place in models of community education outside mainstream education, perhaps within the context of pre-school groups or Saturday schools. These models of parental involvement are not necessarily inappropriate within health education and health promotion in schools, but confrontation and conflict will be more likely to occur if there is a lack of consensus between parents and teachers, and especially if different agendas arise.

It seems equally important that a school should consider the nature of involvement from the point of view of parents. Although parents' attitudes will vary, Pugh (1989), drawing on the results of a three-year study exploring the notion of partnership between parents and professionals in pre-school services, points to the following crucial factors:

- parents need options in the range of participation;
- parents need information as a basis for discussion;
- parents need to be listened to and to be taken seriously.

Health education, and health promotion in particular, has the potential to ameliorate any tensions and differences between school and home, if only because all parties are motivated by an interest in the well-being of the pupil rather than being urged on by a commitment to any particular ideology. For example, whether one is politically to the left or the right on the educational spectrum should not be an issue, although the priorities and means of resourcing will probably be affected by such a position. Ideally, in a truly humanitarian and caring society the health of a child should be placed above the social and political factors which may influence relationships.

Educationalists and health professionals generally agree that the supportive role of parents in any aspect of a child's personal and social development and welfare is crucial to the effective implementation of any health-promoting policy. Despite this fundamental acknowledgement, the role of parents is not exploited as fully as it could be. There is everyday evidence that although schools think they are successfully involving parents in their work, the nature of the involvement and indeed, the relationship with parents, is more often less effective than it could be. This is particularly true in the case of health education, which depends greatly on the nature of parental involvement being a partnership. In believing this to be the case, parents, governors and teachers should work together with health and welfare professionals in order to promote the health of primary pupils.

As part of the welfare network, schools directly participate in and co-ordinate a range of health-promoting activities. In addition, schools have the organisational structure and the facilities to arrange and host the planning groups, subcommittees and parent-teacher meetings that can spearhead health-promoting activities.

Getting Started

For the primary school to be health promoting it needs to work in partnership with parents. It is unlikely that parents will initiate the partnership and therefore the onus lies on the school. The school should therefore declare its desire to work with parents and this declaration should be made clear in the school prospectus and in the school's policy for health education.

In preparing for what is in effect a mission statement, schools need to begin from the premise that in general, parents regard the well-being of their child as being of the utmost importance. In 1992 a number of primary schools in Northfield, Birmingham, as part of the preparation for the creation of a meaningful and relevant school report, conducted a survey among parents in order to discover what parents most wanted to know about their child's progress in school. Almost without exception, information about the child's personal and social development vied with, or took precedence over, the child's academic progress. Many schools were thereby encouraged to begin their official end of year reports to parents with such information. It is likely that if this exercise were to be repeated throughout the country the results would be the same. Lloyd (1990) emphatically supports this view. He comments:

> Ask parents, governors and teachers what they expect of schools, and besides 'good' examination results, literacy and numeracy, they will state that they want young people

to leave school able to:

● express opinions confidently
● be self reliant
● be self disciplined
● take responsibility
● make choices within a moral context
● have clear values and attitudes
● be able to co-operate with others
● make and sustain relationships
● have healthy lifestyles
● be safe.

It does not come as a surprise to any parent or sensitive teacher that a child in a good state of health and with high personal esteem will generally do well and achieve all that is expected of it at school. Most parents want to support the development of their child, but this can take place only if the school is committed to working with parents, and if the ethos of the school demonstrates that fact. It is simply not enough for the school to declare such intentions and then act to the contrary, i.e. inviting parents to help in the classroom and then sending them to a side room for their tea-break! Such action makes quite clear to the parents what the terms of their involvement are and how their status within the school is perceived. Similarly, the attitude, 'support us in our fund-raising, join us as partners in supporting your child to read, but do not bother the class teacher without first making an appointment', will not encourage parents to share views and concerns with teachers; nor will it lead to parental involvement in any other role the school may have in mind.

The nature of the school's declared intent both for health education and promotion and partnership with parents should be uppermost in the mission statement. However, before producing the statement, the school could discover what the views, concerns and priorities of parents are for health and, out of the response, invite parents to contribute to the mission statement. Danai (1994) demonstrates the usefulness of this approach in her case-study (see Chapter 8). The response could also enable the school to identify high-profile areas of health to be targeted, which could form the basis for a future health promotion action-plan. A simple letter with a questionnaire highlighting areas of health such as those identified in *National Curriculum Guidance 5* (1990b), would signal a school's aims and invite comment. Following this, a meeting could be arranged by the school in order to discuss the way forward, either for health education in broad terms or for a specific aspect of children's health which is considered by all to be of current importance. This is an ideal opportunity for the school to discover what the health issues might be for the community – i.e. safe areas for children to play, drug abuse, inadequately maintained housing and dangerous roads.

Health professionals should be invited to participate in the process, for they too have a role in the spirit and actuality of partnership. They also have knowledge and access to health provision beyond the scope of the school. The partnership between teachers and parents could easily facilitate a parallel agenda for addressing health needs within the community – an important concept of the health-promoting school as identified in the *European Network of Health-Promoting Schools Project*, HEA (1993). A working group could be established, consisting of parents, teachers, governors and health professionals, whose aim would be to produce the mission statement, to shape the school's policy for health and to establish an action plan. In addition, the terms of reference for the working group could include the mechanisms for reporting to the general body of the school and for accessing the opinions of teachers and parents not directly involved in the meetings. If this can be achieved, the school is on the way to becoming not merely a 'health friendly' school, but a health-promoting school.

The Role of the Governing Body

There is increasing evidence to suggest that the 'boundaries' that might once have surrounded schools are fading. This process is perhaps being accelerated by a growing acceptance that schools really are part of the whole welfare network. As a result, schools and parents have common concerns and responsibilities regarding the health of their children, and legislation such as the Education Act (1981), the Education Act (1988) and The Children Act (1989) make it impossible for either party to ignore issues of accountability in relation to children's health.

Those for whom direct accountability for the curriculum and overall management of the school is legislated are members of the governing body. Their primary concern is the oversight of the curriculum and thereby, along with HMI and OFSTED, to ensure that schools are not self-regulating bodies. The management role under LMS, and its function as a decision-making body, are now the driving forces of schools and are capable of determining the success or failure of the institution and its organisation. The governing body now has power as well as influence. Schools whose success is determined by how effective they are in delivering what are regarded as high standards in the quality of teaching, learning and relationships are usually those where governors are actively involved, often alongside parents.

Governors can and should offer not merely support and encouragement but also leadership and direction. This is not only possible but also desirable and does not detract from the management role, professional knowledge and skills of the teacher. Governing bodies usually have head teacher members and certainly teacher representatives; if the school is not grant-maintained, LEA advisers are available to give advice and guidance when required and there are also parent members, who generally have the educational interests of their child, and that of others, as the main reason for their commitment. Many also have members with a wide range of experiences, capabilities and professional skills and insights useful to the school. Most members will come from the community in which the school exists and whose members it serves. The governing body therefore has the power to shape decisions not only for the school but in a wider constituency of community interests.

The health education agenda is not merely a school agenda but also a community one and indeed, with health targets set for the nation, clearly a national one. Schools, both as communities themselves and as part of a wider community, have a duty to reflect a balance of local interests. Health education, therefore, is a common ground in which teachers, parents, governors, pupils and members of the local community can meet with health professionals in the interests of everyone. Health education can, perhaps more readily than any other area of the curriculum, facilitate a wider partnership – that of school and community as well as that of parents and teachers. The governing body has both the influence and the power to act as the intermediary or catalyst for the coalition of interested parties. This can be done not merely through policy formulation for health within the School Development Plan, i.e. as in sex education, but also as the result of a specific health action plan. The plan may be implemented by working parties and sub-committees, through the creation of forums; by allowing the school to be used as a venue for health promotion activities; by requesting support from the local authority and the health authority for health education, and a range of other initiatives (many of them listed below). Although a governing body is responsible only for policy and practice in its own school, the growing collaboration of governing bodies in meeting their training needs under LMS shows that there is great potential for governing bodies to cluster. In so doing they may become more influential and effective in promoting the health of their respective schools and communities.

The governing body of a health-promoting school could reasonably be expected to establish a health promotion dimension that runs throughout the school development plan. The plan would set health targets and, where appropriate, their success criteria, in-service requirements, resourcing (including finance), evaluation criteria and means of monitoring development for the school year ahead.

It may be, however, that before a school can feel confident enough to be pivotal in its community it may have to feel confident in its own internal relationships. This applies as much to the relationship between the governing body and the staff of a school as it does to that between teachers and parents. The governors of a health-promoting school can declare their support for both a health agenda and the well-being of the staff as part of that agenda, by defining a positive approach to the welfare of teachers. This could be in the form of: ensuring good working conditions (this, of course, directly benefits children); a pleasant and hygienic staffroom; guaranteeing non-contact time; a regard for the positive self-esteem of teachers by praising when praise is due; declaring that teachers have an entitlement to attend to family responsibilities and a right to receive medical attention during school time. If health promotion is about valuing people and encouraging people to value themselves, then schools should consider how this can be applied to teachers as well as to parents and pupils. When this is achieved, the chances of the school working in partnership with parents and governors will be greatly enhanced.

The ethos of some schools is one that firmly defines its boundaries, over which parents are invited at specifically convenient times. In this situation, the governing body, through its power to appoint the right people and its influence regarding policy and practice, can facilitate the development of closer relationships between the school and the home. Initially it might not achieve the ideal partnership which is conducive to good health education in practice, but it could help towards a process in which parents and teachers build up trust and understanding and break down reserve and inhibition. Eventually a 'partnership of equals' might be created, in which genuine collaboration can take place. The governing body that sees its duty to parents as being beyond the statutory requirement to report to parents, can direct school and parents towards such an ideal partnership and understanding. Health education can lead the way but there could also be involvements and consequences for other areas of the curriculum, as indicated by John Sayer (1989):

> Parents and governors have been drawn together not just by the required participation of elected parents in the governing body. The duty of governors to report to a meeting of parents represents a further formal link and can best be absorbed in a policy of parental involvement in most of the transactions that constitute a school.

Governors, then, can bring about partnership between parents and teachers, between home and school. They can also facilitate collaboration between the school and the community, particularly in addressing the common concerns and issues of the health of the people – adults and children. Health education, when planned and taught in partnership, has the potential to liberate teaching and learning into an exciting, meaningful and beneficial experience, due to the removal of barriers and the building of relationships that affect the whole learning process. Essentially, through health education, parents can acquire empowerment in their children's education: they can challenge inequalities; insist that entitlements are met; and set an agenda which should cause teachers no anxiety, provided the terms of reference and accountability are clear and set in the common interests of all children and the well-being of the community. For this to come about, open dialogue has to be established amongst all concerned in order that common goals may be set.

Parents, teachers and governors have to exercise responsibility in setting any such goals. There are important contexts for health education which should be observed, and which are explicitly defined in the *Health of the Nation* targets, in NCC *Curriculum Guidance 5* and usually in LEA policies for health education. These contexts invariably support both government targets and NC objectives. These are in addition to parentally defined needs and/or those determined by socio-economic or cultural influences. There is a specific need to exercise responsibility and sensitivity in the area of sex education (see Chapter 5). Governing bodies of primary schools will still have the option to decide whether or not sex education is taught in their school.

Clearly, all concerned will have to consider the needs of primary school children regarding their rights to information about sex, sexuality and human relationships. The risks posed to children who are denied this information must also be addressed. In addition, the legal rights of parents (both to withdraw and teach their children themselves, or not at all if that is the case), and the need to respect the wishes of religious groups who may have strict laws, principles and values, must be taken into account. Governors, parents and teachers should realise that just as they have the means to unite, so may they as easily divide. Hence the need for deliberation, sensitivity and negotiation in the building of the partnership. It can be a complex process, especially where values and attitudes which will be most likely to surface in the promotion of health are concerned.

Health-Promoting Activities – A Whole School Approach

Promoting health education in the primary school does not have to begin with a school policy. In fact, in health education, policy often arises out of practice rather than the other way round, and although a policy is a useful and an essential requirement for any school, having one does not necessarily mean that health education has a high profile – or even one at all. It is often easier to create a policy that arises out of practice than to create a policy without. At some time a policy should be written. The approach may be one in which elements of the curriculum are identified as falling within a health remit and then additions are made (perhaps in the context of NCC *Guidance 5*), or it may be drawing on a range of previous and current experiences of health activities within the primary school curriculum. It is certain that both approaches to policy-making can include and benefit from collusion between parents, governors, teachers and children. This can be facilitated through working groups, consultation exercises, workshops and visits to see health education 'in action'. Such activities should include health promotion officers from the health authority, health advisory teachers, health professionals, others from the welfare agencies and, perhaps above all, those schools who already have a successful and well-established programme of health education. Workloads can be shared and loyalties can be developed as people are put into positions of trust by being given specific tasks and then required to report back. Whether as part of the development of a whole school policy for health education or as an activity which is primarily that of promoting the health and well-being of a pupil, what is central to either policy or practice is the activity itself.

The activity can be best prepared for by asking a number of key questions. These will enable an action plan to be formed that will shape and facilitate the activity and give a clear purpose, direction and starting point to those involved:

1 What will be the purpose of the activity?
2 What is the starting point? (What do pupils/community know and believe? What do they need to know?)
3 What are the central influences affecting pupils'/community belief?
4 What aspects of pupil/community lifestyles is the activity seeking to address?
5 Will the activity have impact on, or relate to, the school environment?

6 Does the activity relate to the school curriculum? If so, to which aspect?

7 What is the 'leadership' role of those involved, i.e. who is teacher, facilitator, tutor, helper, contributor? (Remember the nature of the partnership and its importance in the context of the health-promoting school.)

8 How will learning experiences be organised? i.e. group, class, paired, whole school, school/community, etc?

9 Which personal and social skills is the activity seeking to address and develop?

10 Is the central focus of the activity that of school, family or community?

11 Who will participate in the activity – both learners and supporters?

12 How will the activity affect the school/community ethos?

13 How will monitoring and evaluation of the activity take place?

14 How will the final outcomes support school/community development?

The following health activities are examples of opportunities that all the interested parties in the promotion of health in – and through – the primary school may engage in:

- Setting up a Health Project Week for the school to present to the community.
- Open forum for parents, teachers and governors to discuss health issues.
- Questionnaire and meetings to establish health curriculum priority areas.
- Viewing of health resources, i.e. films, texts, artefacts.
- Parents and children come together for a presentation/discussion, e.g. mothers and daughters meet with teachers and school nurse to discuss the on-set of menstruation, and the facilities in the school for meeting girls' needs and boys' needs regarding sexuality.
- Parents, with school support, run a healthy tuck shop.
- Parents work alongside teachers in the classroom during health projects.
- Parents, teachers and pupils, alongside a health or safety professional, prepare a questionnaire or video for use in the home or school.
- Parents are directly involved in the assessment of their children's health work, evaluating the impact of the health curriculum on the home and pupil.
- Community Health Event, planned by the school (including governors and parents) and involving the range of agencies and professionals that would normally support the health needs of the community.
- School establishes support groups for smoking, weight loss, stress, parenting skills (i.e. for dealing with adolescent behaviour, children with difficult behaviour, etc.).
- School hosts a health conference.
- Keep fit classes for parents, teachers and pupils.
- Create a health resource/data bank.
- Food and nutrition event involving the school nurse, dietician, dental hygienist and school meals service.
- Child health 'workshops', perhaps focusing on different age groups including pre-schoolers and teens sessions.
- Establish a school and community health base/centre/room.
- A regular programme of presentations by health and welfare professionals.
- Establish links with agencies and hospitals that care for the elderly; set up a visiting scheme for pupils, parents and teachers.
- Host regular First Aid/Emergency Aid courses, supported by St John's Ambulance or the Red Cross.

- Create local health trails, either based on nutrition (a visit to various local shops and restaurants looking at nutritional value of foods available in the local community) or on identifying local health centres, surgeries, dentists, hospitals (and their specialist areas, such as geriatric, orthopaedic, etc.) ambulance stations and other places which provide health care.
- Organise health and safety audits.
- Hold residential health and fitness weekends.

Good health education and promotion in schools is determined by a range of factors, not least of which are good relationships between governors, staff, parents and pupils, and positive links between the school, family and community. Relationships, though, are not brought about as the result of declarations (perhaps referring to mutual respect, valuing the individual and positive self-esteem). Relationships, in terms of health education, are developed through understanding gained from experiences and activities aimed particularly at developing healthy lifestyles. Support and commitment for these relationships between school, family and community may need to come, initially, from the school and the senior management in particular, with clear intentions of developing productive outcomes for the health of teachers, pupils and parents – and the wider community. The aims should seek to address not merely the immediate health needs but also the future well-being of all concerned. How pupils will react to the decisions they will need to make about their health will to a large extent be determined by the manner in which adults behave towards each other and in relation to their own health. If teachers, parents and governors sincerely care about the health of each other and the pupils of the school, then the manner by which they indicate this and the actions they take, will demonstrate to pupils of the school and to the wider community the role model they set for others to learn from. It should be nothing less than inspirational.

CHAPTER 4

Management of Health Issues: Exercise, Nutrition and Smoking

Norman Scott

Introduction

The concept of the health-promoting school is one which could challenge the very nature of our schooling and address fundamental questions about education itself. On the other hand, it could reinforce narrow and prescriptive views regarding behaviour, control and power. If health education is seen as an empowering process the role of schools is an all-embracing one that seeks actively to support the decision-making process. It can accomplish this through providing opportunities to develop personal autonomy and an understanding of political, economic and social factors that influence health choice. A key feature of an educational role is to recognise the contribution of the educational process itself to the achievement of curriculum aims. A curriculum that purports to support truth, self-esteem and autonomy is at odds with a process that is prescriptive, dogmatic, moralising or even manipulative and dealing in half-truths. The process itself should be healthy and empowering.

Conflicting Values, Health and Education

A health issue, particularly a sensitive one, is often seen as possessing particular characteristics and as such is treated in a different way from other areas of the curriculum. The issues can be identified by the way they challenge an individual's or a group's lifestyle. In the case of young people, an added challenge is in the way in which their health behaviour is perceived by adults. Illegal drugs use, child abuse and sexual behaviour may spring to mind as being contentious, but few things are more precious to us than what we eat, personal legal substance use, and our perceptions of what it is to be fit and healthy. Moreover, health issues are of concern to the general public, to health authorities, and to government and we are therefore affected by the varied and conflicting responses and needs of these groups. Health issues launch themselves into the murky waters of school accountability, bringing with them the baggage of differing opinions and beliefs. How are schools to manage their approach to controversial health issues amidst the uncertainties of society's response? Kogan (1985) writes,

> Values themselves become a context in which other factors affecting policies are grounded. Values are implicit in the power and institutional relations which are both the contexts and the results of different value positions.

Schools, because of the more recent education reforms that have heralded local management, open enrolment, testing, league tables, governor power, parent power and a prescribed curriculum, are now much more aware of these external pressures and demands. Political, economic and social values now more than ever provide a volatile context for school decision-making. The tension between accountability and a school's responsiveness provides an uncertain and increasingly political background to the development of whole school policies that have their ultimate outcomes in health behaviour. Exercise, nutrition, smoking and alcohol programmes all tread this line between coercion and choice, between education and instruction, individual wants and rights and community needs. Despite the many changes in education since the 1988 Education Reform Act, and the resulting pressures on the curriculum, educational debate around health education and whole school policies has grown. This can be explained by government policies that have been keen to see schools adapt their curriculum to the needs of the economy rather than operate as an academic island. So education is seen to benefit through contact with the world of work, e.g. work experience, schools/industry links and compacts.

The school ethos and organisation has also been identified as influential. In areas such as equal opportunities it is possible to influence attitudes and behaviour by the values expressed in all the interactions that take place in schools. Similarly, managing health issues requires a school to clarify its values and to consider how they are promoted in their external relationships. They must also examine the internal organisation and structures to ensure that practice matches policy. Inevitably this examination will require schools to consider the client relationship and accountability. To whom are schools accountable; to parents, pupils or the government?

> Almost too much is known about the 'public life' of institutions – how they should be planned, managed, funded and organised – and too little is understood about the 'private life' – how they work to educate people, how they successfully transmit social and cultural values, how they model the conduct of modern society. Yet it is in this second context of institutions as moral entities, that the most important issues of accountability, responsiveness and responsibility arise. (Scott 1992)

Similarly, the real experiences found within the community, the environment and industry are also seen as opportunities to influence pupils' values and attitudes, to prepare them for their place in society. These policies also open up school practice to society's attitudes and values in ways not previously encountered. Moreover, these attitudes and values are continually changing. One of the issues for schools is, do they lead, do they follow or do they ignore this dynamic process? Or is there a case for placing themselves carefully on the fence, as 'safe' as possible from the hurly burly of conflicting values?

Tannahill (1994) identifies three types of health promotion:

Health Education: communication aimed at enhancing well-being and preventing or diminishing ill-health in individuals and groups through favourably influencing the knowledge, beliefs, attitudes and behaviour of all those in the school and community.

Prevention: the prevention or risk reduction of the illness, injury, disability, handicap or some other unwanted state or event.

Protection: legal or fiscal controls, other regulations or voluntary codes of practice which are aimed at the prevention of ill-health or the positive enhancement of well-being.

Within the curriculum these approaches overlap and interact with pupils and staff in a complex mix. Each of these approaches has its own set of values and its own supporters who are continually promoting their approach as the answer to a problem. Each of these models can be seen to parallel school roles and teaching methods. Protection can be seen as a form of control. In schools this is supported with rules and regulations from washing hands to the legal requirements of health and safety. Prevention can be seen as a form of care where schools are used as a setting to target a client group (children), and so we have schools facilitating medical screening. Finally, health education itself which is based on a model of teaching and learning. Prevention and protection can be seen primarily as part of socialisation – supported by training and the reinforcement of habits. Health education, though, moves to an approach which emphasises awareness and understanding through knowledge, skills, and value clarification, leading to a decision-making stage. Primary schools display all these health features and primary aged children are clearly experiencing all these various approaches.

A health-promoting school would therefore seek to reconcile these as part of a whole school approach within a framework of educational values supported and promoted by the school. A whole school, whole curriculum approach was certainly given legitimacy with the arrival of the NCC Cross Curricular themes and Curriculum Guidance 5 Health Education in 1990, but even here it was seen as important because of its commitment to the economic well-being of the country.

People's health is one of the most important products that any society can create and one of the most important resources required for the creation of any other kind of wealth. (NCC 1990)

Against this background, nutrition, exercise, alcohol and smoking raise some common problems for schools in managing change as part of a whole school approach. Each also brings particular issues and dilemmas for primary school practice. In examining this framework for the provision of policy and practice it is necessary to deal with some specific problems that arise from each of these issues.

A School's Response

Schools address health issues in two main arenas.

1. A whole curriculum response.
2. Interaction of school and the wider community in relation to health behaviour.

The two are both inter-related and dependant on each other. An effective curriculum programme should provide links to real experiences and real decision-making and can influence the relationship between school and community.

Thus a smoking education programme may include material for pupils to take home which could influence parents to change their smoking behaviour. A more planned approach might be a nutritional healthy eating project bringing parents and pupils together to make healthier packed lunches. An exercise trail developed by a school may be made available for community use.

On the other hand, the school's curriculum programme may wish to identify alcohol as a powerful drug but the casual attitude by parents towards alcohol and young people's use may undermine this approach.

Similarly, schools may identify in their approaches to healthy eating the need to recognise the reality of a multi-cultural society and provide opportunities to learn about food from a variety of cultures. The reasons for doing this may not be easily accepted as important or necessary by the wider community, and could be considered as interfering in a family's eating habits and lifestyle.

Competition may be seen by the school as limiting the exercise opportunities for less physically able children and it may take steps to change this by positive discrimination in the school teams. The community may see this as less important than winning and consequently fail to support the school 'teams' and even their own children!

Alcohol

Initially schools will need to determine whether they should include health issues as part of their planned curriculum.

For example, is alcohol a health issue we should be addressing in primary school? What are the criteria we use to make these decisions? What is usually short-lived and of little benefit is a 'crisis' response to a particular incident. This can often serve to distance the issue from mainstream work. The following criteria regarding a particular health issue should be considered:

1 pupil experience and knowledge (listening to children);
2 teachers' knowledge of environment/background of pupils;
3 teachers' knowledge and experience of child development;
4 research in this area;
5 an awareness of wider national initiatives and policies.

Research by J. Balding (1993) and Lloyd, Bennett and Lawrence (1994) suggests that many children have experimented with alcohol before the age of eleven, and that this experience is usually with parental approval. Few would disagree that children through the media and their own experiences, will have 'caught' a vast amount of information about alcohol before eleven and already have firmly held attitudes. The curriculum would therefore need to address these experiences and influences. Consequently, a greater understanding of alcohol use at times of celebrations, and positive responses by adults, would provide a balance to the easily recognised negative aspects of alcohol. It is of equal importance for pupils to have some insights into and awareness of issues such as how gender effects attitudes to alcohol, how different cultures view alcohol, and how the media deals with alcohol in both advertising and in programmes.

A whole curriculum response to alcohol will include the formal curriculum where alcohol as 'our favourite drug' (Balding 1989) should, along with tobacco and medicinal drugs, provide opportunities for a rational and non-judgemental approach which will serve as a basis for drugs education. Of equal importance is the need to examine decision making skills, inter-personal skills, assertiveness, relationships and self-worth. A solid, honest foundation at primary school in drugs education, including alcohol, and a consideration of wider whole school issues will provide valuable insights into the way society responds to illegal drugs. This will require from teachers an approach that recognises the conflicting viewpoints of society.

For schools it will require a clear understanding of how the school values relate to the consideration of alcohol in the wider community. Inconsistencies are not to be ignored. Schools and pupils need to be aware of these inconsistencies, why they exist, and to examine how they might be dealt with.

A sight at many school fairs is the young person with their prize from the tombola, a bottle of cheap wine! The school in other circumstances would frown at children under the age of eleven being given a drug which while not being illegal to drink is illegal for them to buy. What sort of experience is this for pupils? Similarly, schools need to consider how and when alcohol is offered to parents and staff in a variety of situations. The school dance, the cheese and wine evening, the end of term celebration need to be considered in the light of sensible drinking and the messages they give to children. Unlike smoking, the causal relationship between alcohol and serious illness is not explicit, but the legal repercussions from staff drinking alcohol and then being responsible for pupils is very real (Lloyd, Bennett and Lawrence 1994). From a health-promoting school point of view the quality and health of your staff, as your most expensive resource, is vital. The causes and effects of too much alcohol drinking need to be addressed through a caring and protective policy. However, the nature and balance of these particular measures and approaches will depend on a consensus amongst the key groups of:

1 attitudes and awareness to alcohol as a social drug;
2 attitudes towards children as individuals;
3 parents and staff sensitivities towards each other's use of alcohol;
4 teaching approaches which are sensitive and non-judgemental rather than those which give simplistic warning messages;
5 the role of adults as models of behaviour to young people.

Nutrition

How are we to provide a whole curriculum response to health issues so that stated whole school values and aims match policy and practice?

If we use nutrition as an example this would link up the following areas:

1 the classroom teaching about food and drink;
2 the school meals/lunchtime experience;
3 the school response to sweets and drinks as rewards;
4 the school tuck shop;
5 the approach to food out of school (school trips);
6 the eating habits and behaviour of adults in the school.

All these areas represent some aspect of protection and prevention but the pivotal response and conclusions for schools must be in the process of health education.

How can we provide opportunities and support for real experiences in decision-making both in school and the wider community?

This would include all the previous points but would also require some response from and to parents – particularly over packed lunches, sweets and school dinners. Most importantly, schools need to promote the interest and motivation for parents and the wider community to take part in this process. It will require negotiation with the school meals service (where these still exist) to provide alternative healthy choices.

The dilemma for school is how far to go in prescribing certain behaviour and in controlling the environment, and how does this match the educational aims of developing choice and autonomy and preparing pupils for the real world.

1 How are cultural sensitivities around food dealt with in the classroom?
2 How are the feelings of the children (and their families) with perceived weight problems managed?
3 Does the tuck shop provide only healthier alternatives or does it provide both healthy and less healthy choices? If it provides less healthy choices is there a pricing policy in favour of the healthier choices?
4 What is the process that both develops awareness and provides support for pupils to explore a choice between wants and needs? To bridge the gap

between the two could be seen as a curriculum aim which will ensure the successful operation of a healthier choice system at school meals.

5 Does the school ban all extra food, drinks and sweets or is the ban on only the less healthy sweets and not on fruit?

6 Does a thought-out policy extend to the reward system or is this forgotten as sweets, chocolate bars, etc, are given out to the 'good' and 'successful'?

If schools are to implement a healthy eating policy the formal curriculum must provide means by which pupils not only understand the need for a balanced diet but actually have opportunities to extend and try out a more varied diet. If this is supported at home then a policy related to the tuck shop and school meals may prove workable. However, will schools have the time or the resources to persevere for results? The school meals service is dependent on the customer for survival. If customer numbers drop because pupils don't get what they want then the service, and jobs, will be at risk.

In both policy and practice such a programme must complement other behaviour-related and organisational policies which have wider implications for health, personal and social education, and behaviour policies. Whole school policies need to consider the implications of the formal taught curriculum and staff behaviour and also how the external environment impinges on these areas and how this should be managed.

How does the programme reach out to the wider community and how does it manage and involve the community in school?

What is the policy when the special needs support teacher comes along with sweets to motivate children with learning difficulties? What is the response if the police involve the school in a competition which, if children enter, automatically means they win a token for a free chocolate bar?

Perhaps even more insidious are those factors relating to Local Management of Schools (LMS) where schools responsible for their own budget can easily produce a situation where money raised is not related to the whole curriculum and where the generation of funds is considered more important than the health messages. Commercial companies, particularly those with products aimed at the youth culture, are not slow in seeking marketing opportunities. What is the school's response to the provision of a fizzy drinks machine which earns a large profit? Commercial interests and values are held in such high esteem that they are difficult for schools to resist. Are schools pressured by this client relationship into seeing marketing as a means to a commercial end rather than marketing the ideals and values of education and schools?

If there was consensus by parents, the school staff and the school meals service for a healthy, balanced choice the efforts to respond by schools would have far more support. However, without this consensus and with schools and the school meals service more inclined to be sensitive to pupil wants and commercial interests, the line of least resistance is an option that many schools will find attractive. The result may be a curriculum that does not take account of differing values, and prescribes a 'correct' formal curriculum response which is divorced from the real decision-making, so failing to provide opportunities to challenge attitudes and behaviour in the wider school community.

It can be argued that the social, economic and political factors involved in addressing behaviour around eating and other health issues are both complex and (despite all efforts) often outside the influence of the schools.

Is it worth the effort? Will these sorts of policies actually make a difference to the health behaviour of young people? Is the evaluation of such policies measured in behaviour outcomes? If we do justify our policy in terms of health behaviour how will this take account of other equally important factors in personal and social education? Is it more important for a young person to feel confident and have a high self-esteem, or to be instructed to eat the 'right' food.

What is essential is that important holistic messages are not lost in a desire to see 'good' and 'healthy' promoted. Eating should be fun – an enjoyable activity as well as one that provides nutrition. If young people are continually worried about their diet and the way they look, or have a fear of food and eating, this is just as unhealthy as indulging in vast amounts of fatty foods. A balanced approach and a balanced diet should ensure policies that are not self-defeating or counter productive.

The aims for a policy should include:

- an understanding of the link between diet and lifestyle, (where changing and sometimes uncertain information is to be expected);
- opportunities to celebrate and enjoy the variety of foods from different culture and countries;
- opportunities for decision-making, choice and responsibility.

Strategies and action should take place in the whole curriculum to ensure this policy is implemented. However, monitoring and evaluation of the policy should not over-emphasise changes in pupils' eating habits. It should focus on how confident pupils are in making decisions and in explaining their choices.

Exercise

Exercise is bound up with health in innumerable ways and over the last 25 years has been confirmed as the way to achieve health. Exercise programmes from Jane Fonda to the Green Goddess, special exercise equipment...that stretches and pulls, that allows you to step up...all promise to make you look good and feel good. Taking exercise and being fit is seen as an essential part of being healthy. Health and exercise have almost become synonymous.

Similarly, the attitude towards physical education in schools, with its own traditions and agendas, will also influence a school's view of health and exercise. If there is such a close relationship between exercise and health then we would expect fewer conflicts and confusions in developing a school policy. However, being fit does not mean being healthy. Almond describes health as:

a state of enjoying realisation of potencies in bodily design and function whereas fitness has some extrinsic goal, usually a performance as its object. This makes the body and its condition a means to an end. (Almond 1987)

Perhaps a question to ask at this point is, 'can exercise be harmful to health?'

Clearly, we can recognise harmful exercises and too much exercise. This is a matter of technical knowledge and relies on an understanding of the effects of exercise on the body. This is very important both to understand and to get right. Too often exercises are inappropriate for the task, for the age and physical condition of the people involved, or are carried out at the wrong time, in the wrong place or in the wrong order. This also includes games exercises where the pressures to ignore these considerations are great. Children are also asked to exercise without any choice or to exercise without any understanding of purpose.

A sense of proportion can disappear as children are inculcated into the 'spirit' of games and team sports. The weather may be cold and wet but enduring such conditions is seen to build character. How much does this help pupils to remain positive and motivated with regard to exercise?

A dress code dating from the last century or constant demands by schools for specialised sportswear may prove influential in determining children's attitudes towards games and exercise. An aggressive, competitive male orientated approach will soon deliver a message to girls that this area of the curriculum is not for them.

How are schools to ensure that a curriculum programme promoting exercise is contributing to and supporting health?

For a whole curriculum response there is a need to ensure that exercise is seen by all children as a fun activity with a purpose. The process needs to ensure that differing needs are identified and met in order to ensure participation and a feeling of self-worth. Enjoyment must be seen by the pupils as important, and consequently be a part of any evaluation. The curriculum must also develop the understanding of the relationship between exercise and body fitness. A combined and balanced approach of exercise and relaxation allied to a positive process will support mental and physical health. If this approach was applied to all pupils as individuals then all children, not only the physically able, would find opportunities for success.

Further choice is often provided by primary schools in extra curricular activities, either by the schools themselves or by links to community activities. The problem with many extra curricular activities is that they can often be elitist, producing teams to win or providing support and success only to the more able. This may be in conflict with stated school values in relation to exercise in the planned curriculum. However, these extra curricular activities can be a more powerful influence on pupils' attitudes to exercise than any classroom approaches. They are also the part of a school exercise programme that impacts on the wider school community and consequently may be an area that requires a more active 'selling' of school values related to participation, individual needs, tolerance and self-worth.

Smoking

Smoking is in itself a 'drug war'. The combatants are identified, battle lines drawn and regular salvoes are fired – research, statistics, campaigns and media – at each other and at the public. In responding with whole curriculum approaches schools inevitably find themselves drawn into the war-zone! No one at the moment expects a school policy to insist that staff take exercise or eat only 'healthy' food. Yet the Health Education Authority (HEA) expect schools to move towards smoke free environments (*Towards a Smoke Free Generation*, HEA 1991). The rationale is based on the wealth of information now available on the health implications of smoking and passive smoking. The carrot and stick approach of benefits to pupils and staff and threats of litigation if clean air is not provided are key strategies in the development of such policies (*Towards a Smoke Free Generation* HEA 1991). Health concerns linked to smoking have produced a number of public health measures, such as health warnings on cigarette packets, new legislation on selling cigarettes and some advertising control on TV. However, when these measures are considered inadequate, educational responses are seen as imperative. The pressures to achieve results through education also influence the approaches. On attending a seminar on some new anti-smoking material aimed at young people, it was stated that the material was significant for 'its use of all the media tricks seen in young people's magazines and advertising'. When it was suggested that this approach would or should be challenged and scrutinised in much the same way as other material that exploits and manipulates in order to influence behaviour, the response from the producers of the material was that 'the end justified the means'! Clearly a dangerous route for schools and education to go down.

Health targets and health agendas could possibly be so demanding that the methods used put in jeopardy the internal validity of education itself.

One of the *Health of the Nation* targets in relation to cancer is, 'to reduce smoking prevalence among 11-15 year olds by at least 33% by 1994' (*Health of the Nation* 1992). Schools and education should consider carefully their role in such a policy.

Scott (1992) describes the cultural responsibility of education as, 'the allegiance to rationality, truth and knowledge, which all those engaged in education must accept.' He goes on to say that,

> Education at all levels must be responsible in this primary and fundamental sense before its accountability to the state, the market place or society can have any special significance. For without this primary responsibility education would be truly a dead world. Its external utility is rooted in its internal validity, its private integrity. (Scott 1992)

Developing whole school smoking policies for primary schools certainly makes sense for all the reasons associated with health, passive smoking and role model behaviour. Providing a smoke-free working environment is an achievable objective. However, what is important is the way the policy is developed and supported. The formal curriculum, the informal curriculum and the ways policies reach out to parents must provide positive support to smokers and positive images of people who smoke or have smoked. Parents who smoke can still be loving, provide a caring environment and are not going to die next week! The development of relationships through understanding and empathy is a key to enhanced self-esteem and decision-making. This must be a priority for a school programme rather than simplistic scare-mongering that confuses, blames and instils guilt.

Smoking also challenges views on the scope and effectiveness of health education. How do we account for the increases in smoking behaviour, despite all the known health risks and all the media and educational campaigns? The view that health education is simply a matter of personal choice once the facts are known, skills learned and attitudes clarified is shown to be only part of the story. Smoking and other health issues clearly reflect the need to address political, social and economic factors in relation to health behaviour. Smoking has reduced when prices are higher and increased when prices in real terms have decreased (HEA 1992). The increases in young women smoking suggest that we need to address gender and cultural influences. The capability to demonstrate knowledge and skills in one situation (a classroom) is altered dramatically in a different scenario.

Conclusions

It could be argued that for issues where other factors have a more direct impact on health behaviour, education is less important. So why bother? This argument, based on measurable outcomes and value for money which supports prevention and protection models of intervention, could possibly deny to schools the opportunity of enabling young people to take part in a process that will prepare them for adult life.

Nowhere else in the primary school curriculum do we select content or evaluate based on specific individual pupil behaviour in three or four years' time. Maths, science, art, music, history and geography are not taught to pupils with the expectation that they will all become scientists or not become scientists, as in not become smokers. Health issues should not be about 'not smoking, not eating unhealthy food' but should focus on the positive. What is important is a holistic positive health message about valuing oneself and others and an awareness of political, economic and social issues that impact on health behaviour – a process that will enable future citizens to challenge the *status quo*. There is no reason why media, gender and economic issues cannot be part of the primary curriculum, and pupils should be aware of how these influence their health behaviour and affect the people and organisations around them.

Health issues, because of their sensitivity, demand approaches by teachers that are considerate of pupils' cultures, individual needs, relationships and economic circumstances. Methods are required that support an ethos that builds confidence in pupils and which enables them to participate and teachers to listen. The

National Curriculum Council, *Curriculum Guidance 5: Health Education*, with no clear remit to comment on methodology, nevertheless goes on to say:

> If a health education programme is to help pupils make informed choices, establish a health lifestyle and build up a system of values, the teaching methods used are as important as the content of the lessons.

This powerful statement recognises that a school's main tasks of teaching and learning provide real opportunities for education in healthy decisions. This is supported by identifying 'ground rules' as a useful classroom method to build confidence and trust which will enable more sensitive work to continue.

If health issues both present and in the future are to be dealt with seriously in primary schools this consideration of teaching and learning styles and development of a classroom ethos which enables pupils and teachers to deal with sensitive subjects is essential. A non-judgemental approach is needed that will allow pupils to explore the various attitudes and differences which influence people's opinions and decisions. These influences are there in everyone's life – culture, tradition, up-bringing, experiences, and religion.

The curriculum in relation to health issues has a socialisation role which would include aspects of protecting and preventing ill health. However, the main task is teaching and learning both about this environment, and within it, the role of the learner as an individual, as a member of a group, and of the wider community. The decisions made in this environment are based on values inherent in political, social and economic structures. The curriculum should actively seek to enable the pupil to influence and challenge this context. The conclusion of this approach is a curriculum that is dynamic and sensitive in responding to community health needs and concerns, but the means by which these needs and concerns are addressed is firmly based on an educational rationale. This approach will require clear policies and a promotion of educational values, otherwise we will see health education in schools become increasingly issue based, driven by health targets, supporting short-lived projects low in developmental learning approaches but high in public relation opportunities.

An understanding and a partnership between school, education, health and the wider community in relation to health issues should lead to a shared agenda to enable and empower. However, this alliance needs to recognise the responsibility and accountability of the school setting and so co-operate to ensure the 'good health' of the system which it seeks to employ.

CHAPTER 5

The Route to Sexual Health - Taking Children by the Hand and Leading them Safely Along

Diana Veasey

> We end our trek along the difficult path of vulnerability with accounts of two children who have trod the path before us. One continued climbing, and one fell by the wayside. They have left us two messages on behalf of all children: The first is, 'You are big, make the path smoother', the second is, 'I will walk, but hold my hand.' If we fail to rise to these two challenges, we had better cease to think of ourselves as anything we or our children could ever remotely, possibly admire. (Konner 1991)

Introduction

Year on year teachers are inescapably reminded of one outcome of sexual activity as each new cohort of children begins its passage through the education system. Yet in spite of intense media obsession with sex, it is not a topic easily fitted into adult-child conversation. Why is it so subject to 'adult' censorship? When adults reflect on their own experience of sexuality then check out what they *think* they know, they become aware of prejudices acquired and peculiarities of understanding which it may be wrong or misleading to pass on. Children need to be nurtured, shown which way to go, and protected on their journey to becoming sexually healthy adults. Applying Konner's thinking, unless adults are admirable in this respect they will have nothing to offer their children.

What is Sexual Health?

Research reveals no positive definition of sexual health. Instead it may be glimpsed by reading between lines of sexual ills to avoid and by piecing clues together. The emerging jig-saw pictures a balance between physical, mental and spiritual well-being. The experience from birth to death:

a) a body functioning, developing and maturing within a 'normal' sexual pattern, free from sexually transmitted disease or unintended pregnancy, with unmutilated genitals, capable of experiencing full physical sexual pleasure to orgasm, and reproducing its kind;

b) a mind aware of the current stage of its body's sexual development, and having knowledge and understanding to deal with practical implications such as menstruation, nocturnal emissions, personal safety, sexual relationships, personal moral choices, fertility and maintaining sexual health.

c) a spirit able to be, feel, and act sexually from a deeply held positive self-esteem; and able to esteem and respect others' sexual existence, needs and rights. A spirit capable of transcendence. For some people this includes a response to God.

To develop holistically a balance between growth of body, mind, and spirit is critical as are, at their interfaces emotional, moral and cultural experiences. The more intentionally we reflect upon the experiences we encounter, the more learning we achieve, and the greater potential we have assertively to accept or change our destiny. Experiences will be limited by various factors. (Veasey 1993)

What Kind of Limiting Factors Stop People Achieving Sexual Health?

Limiting factors include ignorance, deception, imposition, lack of personal skills and confused messages.

Sexual health within a community depends on each of us understanding 'sexuality' and managing our own sexual expression in the context of other people's. Just as smokers may damage others by imposing secondary smoking, so a promiscuous individual may damage others by imposing a cocktail of bacteria and viruses. Figure 5.1 illustrates more of the complex network which weaves around sexual health.

Much research seems beyond the interests of primary children but does identify sexual health targets. A synthesis signposts the way for health targets to:

- manage fertility;

- avoid sexually transmitted diseases (STDs, sometimes still referred to as 'Venereal Diseases', or now the recently introduced term 'Sexually Transmitted Infections').

Much research risks being partisan. Can people trust research funded by condom or drug manufacturers with a strong marketing interest; inspired by a women's magazine whose sample is biased towards the views of self selected reader-respondents; or obtained from teenagers in doubtfully controlled circumstances where peer pressure may influence responses? How does such research impact on primary schooling bearing in mind age, readiness and progression?

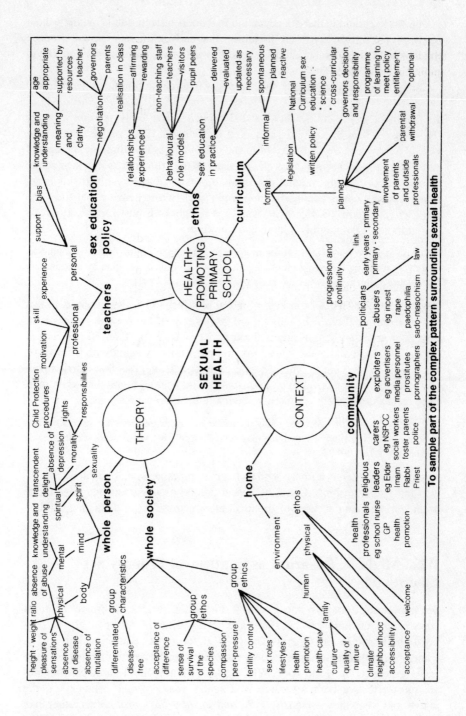

Figure 5.1 The Complex Pattern surrounding Sexual Health

One has to conclude that sex education in schools reflects adults' anxiety about young people's sexuality. 'The 'prejudice' that early sex education will produce children with 'healthy sexuality' is open to serious question.' (Elkind David quoted in Richard 1990)

Children from six to puberty seem to show natural inhibition and be repulsed by sex-talk. Some psychologists believe this 'period of latency' is disturbed to the detriment of the child. Could sexual explicitness in early sex education be classed as official abuse? Franz (quoted in Richard, 1990, p30) suggests that today's adolescents remain largely in the concrete stage of thinking, compared with Piaget's model which cites eleven years as the critical next step, and so are not capable of making rational decisions to protect sexual health. If this is so, unambiguous moral teaching defining 'right' and 'wrong' is essential from primary school to post-16. However, Ann Cale Kruger of Emory University investigated moral reasoning in children and found:

> that an eight year old girl profits more in her development of moral reasoning by actively puzzling through a problem with another eight year old than by working out the same problem under her mother's guidance. (Konner 1991)

Despite constant media exposures of moral blunder, a majority of adults in fact model sexual fidelity. In Britain around 90 per cent of the population sooner or later pursue sexual health targets through marriage. More than 50 per cent of marriages endure and many whose first marriage fails try again with a new partner. Research by 'One to One', Middlesex Hospital, suggests that married people, particularly men, tend to be less stressed and healthier, and that when marriage breaks down there are likely to be major health repercussions.

> Parents' attitudes of which they may themselves be unaware, have an important effect on how children view sex, and this may set a limit to what sex education can achieve. (Jones in White 1989)

So can child-centered primary schools begin to promote sexual health by affirming family relationships? Can they present faithful monogamous marriage as the norm without being accused of 'political incorrectness' or of damaging children with single parents?

What Might be Regarded as Entitlement Primary Sex Education?

Sex education, frequently incorrect and misleading, begins informally amongst peers behind the infamous bike shed and heralds disaster. Alternatively, according to the World Health Organisation (WHO), formal sex education delivered as a universal entitlement can be a powerful tool for sexual health. In nineteen studies of sex education world-wide, WHO concluded that school-based programmes are most effective both when received *before young people become sexually active*, and when they *emphasise skills and social behavioural norms* rather than detached factual knowledge.

In The Netherlands the legal age of consent is now 12 years, and Dutch children begin their sex education in primary school. In spite of pessimistic predictions that such a direct approach would encourage immorality, research indicts a reduction in unintended pregnancies and STD transmission since the programme began and, more significantly, that many young people now choose to delay their sexual experience by several years.

British teenagers complain that they need more help to manage relationships. This is both justification and a golden opportunity for infant and junior teachers to extend and consolidate existing work on self-esteem. Upper primary teachers in co-operation with parents need to prepare pupils for puberty and equip them with skills and materials necessary to manage menstruation, nocturnal emissions, spots, aches and pains. In Autumn 1992 the suicide of a young girl was reported in the newspapers. She had found blood in her underwear. If her sex education had been adequate perhaps she would not have reacted in this fatal way.

Suicide is more often associated with another aspect of sexual health, 'sexuality'. A young person experiencing homosexual feelings in a world constantly reinforcing heterosexuality as the desired norm, may feel rejected and dejected to point of suicidal depression. Only one in one hundred men identify themselves as living an exclusively homosexual lifestyle, though around four percent admit to at least one experimental homosexual experience around puberty, or to experiencing homosexuality as a passing phase (Wellings 1994). Figures are even lower for women, so a self-identified gay man or lesbian will inevitably feel isolated in school, and keep the cause of their misery hidden to avoid censure. Both need reassurance, to recognise the possible transience of their feelings, and to know that there are satisfactory ways of managing life if they do find themselves permanently orientated homosexually. 'Sexuality' as a topic may be more appropriate in secondary schooling, but attitudes and values modelled, supported and developed in primary schools will have a lasting impact.

Positive images depicting difference in gender, race, ability, age and culture can stimulate understanding of equality of worth and power balance. They might make the difference between becoming a bully (rapist?), victim (through alcohol abuse?), or capable of giving other people the 'unconditional positive regard' espoused by Carl Rogers. This is more often described as 'love' by Christian writers, incorporating the four elements of 'charity, Eros, affection, and friendship'. (Lewis, 1963)

A glance through the agony columns in teenage girls' magazines such as *Mizz* and *Just 17* reveals anxieties from boys as well as girls. Relevant primary sex education can eliminate basic worries before teenage years, even for well taught children from practising religious community groups. All young people may experience difficulty in future relationships unless they are given a formal opportunity to explore implications of different customs with friends from other moral and cultural backgrounds who may live as close as next door.

If primary sex education is focused on developing self-esteem, understanding the basic biology of human reproduction and the range of physical variation which is 'normal' (e.g. penis size, age of starting menstruation), respecting

differences of belief, preparing for puberty and the emotional challenge of adolescence, and acquiring skills to avoid early damage to sexual health, then a primary child's entitlement towards effective management of his or her own sexuality is surely delivered.

> ...once the programme is put into action many schools have been greatly relieved and
> delighted to find the children have accepted it readily and unselfconsciously, and seem-
> ingly without the hang-ups of the generation of grown-ups in charge! (Went 1988)

What is the Context of Sex Education for Sexual Health?

Sexual health is set in the context of family, peer group, school and community,
where knowledge and understanding vary according to custom, culture and tradition, and ability. The national norm is a nuclear family with a mother and father
at home, though one classroom may contain many exceptions. An extended family including grand-parents, uncles, aunts, etc, may be further extended by step-
relations, so one child and his or her siblings may be expected to 'own' four sets
of grand-parents. Sustaining so many relationships can be overwhelming, with
double celebrations throughout. In mixed cultural marriages various combina-
tions of Jewish Hanukkah, Islamic Eid, Hindu Diwali and Christian Christmas,
might compete for attention. Different religions may encourage similar sexual
values.

> ...they can speak of God's love and tell how special and precious each human spirit is
> from the moment of its creation; that sex is a wonderful gift and part of the whole amaz-
> ing process of being human. (Veasey 1993,2)

Yet close family members even within one faith group may display different
moral decisions, modelling different sexual attitudes from free expression to lifelong celibacy.

Rarely, British children have two mothers or two fathers in lieu of heterosexual parenting. The practice of homosexuality is not tolerated in most mainstream
religions, nor are bondage, sadomasochism, oral and anal sex, but the secular
world displays other messages. One publication (Lenderyou, 1993) includes
material on menstruation, masturbation, sexual intercourse, STDs including
HIV/AIDS (now increasingly referred to as HIV disease), and oral sex. Another
(Sanders and Swindon 1990) includes worksheets to raise awareness of the
process of full penetrative sex, and a range of contraceptive methods. The amend-
ments to the Education Reform Act 1988 (Education Act 1993) were designed
to eliminate the need to expose children to knowledge of sexual behaviours considered undesirable by many, particularly anal sex (illegal for heterosexual cou-
plings and males under 18 years or non-consenting) which 'jumped' into the curriculum in the early 1990s in response to the high risk it poses for HIV
transmission. Many health educators believe children and young people cannot
protect their sexual health without knowing about it, but what do peers naturally
gossip about?

Children report 'being with friends' as the best part of going to school (Consumers' Association 1993), so a peer-group is arguably the most influential context for sex education. A child's desire to be accepted leads to false claims of conquest to buy attention, gain kudos, and lead others into supposed copycat experiments. Well-informed sex education acceptable to as many parents as possible will avoid them withdrawing their children to leave weak links in peers' sharing of knowledge. Appropriate information and guidance can help children reach a consensus of opinion about how to achieve sexually healthy lifestyles, first within their group, and later within the ethos of their wider community. This might be abstinence.

Perhaps the greatest misunderstanding about abstinence education is the belief that it is religious in nature...however abstinence is also a medical, psychological, sociological, and moral issue. (Richard 1990)

The most effective way to prevent sexual transmission of the virus (HIV) is to abstain from sexual intercourse, or for two uninfected partners to remain mutually faithful. (WHO 57: Global programmes on AIDS statement)

Whole school ethos is significant in promoting or diminishing self-esteem. To overhear, 'People who have anything to do with female circumcision should all be locked up...' said by one teacher to another in revulsion could be devastating. This practice, illegal but still evident in Britain, is central to self-respect in some cultures, although some women of those cultures are now campaigning strongly against it. How might a circumcised girl in the classroom react on hearing this? Her operation cannot be reversed. That is an extreme example. More commonly a discussion of a child's home difficulties in earshot of pupils does damage. Public criticism, added to home abuse, pushes children further down the road to becoming perpetual victims, reacting through bad behaviour or truancy. Sexually abused children may run away from home only to be picked up and further abused by pimps. As prostitutes or rent boys they find economic survival, ironically capitalising on well-rehearsed feelings of social rejection and low self-worth. Inevitably their sexual health suffers.

Research by Sheffield University Department of Psychology indicates that long term effects of bullying are more likely to lead to depression in adult life and to people finding it harder to form adult relationships. Professor Smith's survey of 24 schools involving 7000 children found that 27 per cent of primary school children had been bullied, 12 per cent were bullies, and that bullied children were two to three times more likely to have special educational needs. These figures indicate the importance of establishing and maintaining anti-bullying programmes as a means of improving relationships, and of avoiding a group of children too traumatised to assimilate information essential to the future sexual well-being of themselves and others. Teachers have a professional responsibility towards developing and maintaining a suitably supportive ethos. Their personal bias will have an impact, and so too will their respect for others, and choice of teaching materials as the following examples signal.

Some years ago a television sex education series featured a mother, partner and child, but no wedding ring. This omission caused pain to a number of Christians who complained at the subversive image they felt it offered. Today, strict Muslim girls expect to wear *hijab*, or modest dress, at all times to cover body, limbs and often hair, at least from the time of their menarche (first period) which could occur during their last couple of years at primary school. Modesty is no longer part of mainstream British thinking, judging by media images, but Roman Catholics too emphasise modesty as virtue. Naked bodies in text-books may seem offensive and may block learning because children are protectively withdrawn from lessons by shocked, offended parents.

When cases of abuse, illegal behaviour, estrangement from a significant adult, or bereavement are disclosed the truth of children's distress must be affirmed, and where necessary referral made to outside professionals. Committed Christian, Jewish, Muslim and other religious leaders can provide pastoral support, and are not the handicap to sex education they are sometimes presumed to be. They share a compassionate concern for sexual health, as the co-operative multi-faith work of The Sex Education Forum demonstrates (Thomson 1993).

The last contextual influence on sex education to mention here is that of the media, in the areas of television and advertising. The nine o'clock broadcasting 'watershed' is only loosely adhered to. Trailers for explicit materials are frequently screened pre-watershed, i.e. for films and plays scheduled for screening after it. Snippets of the raunchiest or most violent scenes flash by to encourage a good audience and repercussions can ripple into school.

Television sex is a powerful marketing tool with a side-effect. In recent years young children may have become subconsciously familiar with chocolate bar oral sex, ice-creamy foreplay and an orgasm of after-shave. Bare flesh in showers, scanty underwear and hairy chests are commonplace and, at the onset of puberty full of vanity and insecure sexual self-esteem, teenagers face direct marketing of dubiously performing spot removers; essential purchases of sanitary towels, panty-liners, and tampons competing for brand loyalty from girls who have started menstruation; and a bewildering set of wet and dry options for shaving to confuse newly whiskering boys. Firms supply teaching materials and free samples as a promotional tactic.

Many children now enjoy video access at home, with or without parental assent, to a range of sexual behaviours, so teachers are wise to prepare appropriate responses to deal with playground mimics, or queries arising. Additionally, pornographic computer programmes are swapped through school computer systems and, like drugs, are finding their way into a soft untapped extensive primary school market. Teachers promoting sexual health will want to monitor software and co-operate with outside agencies such as police, health and social workers to contain this spread of illegal materials.

The context for sex education is complex and a great deal of informal sex education is inevitably woven into daily life which can complicate the delivery of formal sex education. So now to the law, and government support.

Which Government Guidances and Legislation Concern Education for Sexual Health in Primary Schools?

Guidance and legislation in 1-2 below applies to maintained schools, though government hopes others will follow the same course; 3-7 below apply to all schools.

1 National Curriculum Orders are legally compulsory in County, Controlled and Grant Maintained schools: KS1/KS2: English (AT1 on listening and speaking) can contribute to initiating and maintaining secure relationships.

Science orders cover naming human body parts, and functioning of major systems and organs.

Other formal sex education is at the discretion of governors. Their legal obligations arising out of the Education Act 1993, effective from September 1994 are:

a) To decide whether or not to provide sex education (in County and Controlled schools in consultation with the Head).
b) To keep an up to date separate written statement:
   i) of their policy including, where appropriate, details of curriculum content and organisation.
   ii) where they conclude sex education should not form part of the curriculum.
c) To make sure that any sex education provided is set within a moral and family value context to ensure the spiritual, moral, cultural, mental and physical development of pupils at school and in society, and prepare them for the opportunities, responsibilities and experiences of adult life.
d) To decide how parents are to be consulted about and informed of policy.
e) To include information about the right of withdrawal and how parents may exercise it (except in voluntary aided and special agreement schools).

2 Guidance on interpretation and implementation of the Education Act with regard to sex education is contained in Circular 5/94. This covers policy and programmes of learning; encourages parent-school co-operation; affirms roles of responsible adults; and an annexe publishes guidance on good practice in developing a sex education policy.
3 The government sets official targets relating to sexual health in its *Health of the Nation* publication, 1992:

- to reduce the incidence of gonorrhoea (an indicator for HIV transmission, and thus AIDS trends) by at least 20 per cent by 1995 (baseline 1990);
- to reduce by at least 50 per cent the rate of conceptions in the under 16's by the year 2000 (baseline 1990) and so reduce the incidence of unintended teenage pregnancy and abortion in that age group.

Primary school sex education can pave the way for secondary sex education which is more focused to meet these targets. *In all maintained secondary schools sex education is compulsory and must include teaching on HIV/AIDS (HIV disease/infection)*, which no longer forms part of the National Curriculum Science at KS3. Parents have been given the right (from September 1994) to withdraw their children from classes where sex education forms a formal component both in primary and secondary schools (Education Act 1993), and must be kept fully informed on how to go about this.

4 On the one hand sexual intercourse is illegal for girls and boys under the age of 16 whether or not they have passed puberty; on the other hand, Judges in the Gillick case (1985) ruled that in exceptional circumstances doctors may prescribe contraceptives for under 16-year olds without parental consent, and without parents being informed, provided their young patients are deemed sufficiently mature to understand the consequences.

Paradoxically, a mature primary pupil could be illegally active sexually, officially on the pill, yet have no right to attend sex education lessons agreed in school policy if her parents have chosen to withdraw her. Those who truant are most likely to miss the classes, yet ironically, in socially deprived areas such as inner cities, be in the most need of early sex education. Teachers approached by a pupil for advice should not trespass on parental rights and responsibilities. The Circular 5/94 states that giving contraceptive advice without parental knowledge or consent would be an 'inappropiate' exercise of teachers' responsibilities. All teachers embarking on sex education are strongly recommended to take their own responsibility for reading, interpreting and acting within guidance in 5/94.

5 Section 28 of the Local Government Act 1988, concerned that local authorities should not promote homosexuality or publish material with the intention of promoting it, continues to provoke anxiety. Homosexuality may not be taught as an alternative family lifestyle but, according to the Sex Education Forum, Circular 12/88 from the then DoE clarifies that Section 28 does not affect schools; and subsequent HMI and DES Guidance states that, 'sensitive, responsible and unbiased discussions of homosexuality are appropriate within sex education.' (Thomson, 1992). Questions should be answered honestly, and pupils' 'need to know' about sexuality met.

6 Homosexual acts are illegal until a man is 18 years old (amended from 21 years in 1994), though pressure groups continue pushing to reduce this age consent to 16 years, to be 'justly' in line with heterosexual legislation. There is no legislation concerning lesbian sex acts. Heterosexual anal sex is illegal.

7 Education (No. 2) Act 1986 requires LEAs to make available free training to governors responsible for formulating sex education policy. LEAs must state their sex education policy, and deal with parental complaints.

What are the Roles of Governors, Teachers and Pupils in the Provision of Sex Education in a Health-Promoting Primary School?

At home:
CHILD   Where do we come from, Mom?
MOM   Jamaica, where your grandparents live. Ask your teacher to show you on the map, son.

At school:
CHILD   Mom says to ask you where I come from?
TEACHER (Who last night did her homework on the mechanisms of sex, and how to present them to her children should they ever ask) Sit down, keep very still, and I will tell you...

Tonight's teacher homework might be to brush up on listening skills, or consider how better to empower parents!

While parents frequently report feeling responsible, research showed that only 7 per cent of parents felt they should provide all necessary sex education for their children, 60 per cent wanted home and school to share, and 27 per cent wanted school to take the whole responsibility. Only 7 per cent of mothers and 2 per cent of fathers felt they had been well educated in sexual health. Although more than 70 per cent of teenagers felt they could discuss most things with parents, sex was not on the agenda (Allen, 1987). Attention to sex education has changed little in recent years, so primary parents are likely to say the same. A significant LWT broadcast 'The inside track of parenting', produced by Beth Miller, 1993, and accompanied by a glossy booklet sponsored by BT, made no mention of parents' role in sex education. However, a number of primary schools have involved parents successfully.

Governors' role is to decide, implement and review policy, usually with guidance from teachers who have to put policy into action. They may seek additional help from community health professionals. Governors will want to ensure that local faith groups are represented, perhaps through their SACRE, but how do teachers feel about the role expected of them?

Some teachers teach with confidence and expertise, but many teachers feel embarrassed. Their own sex education was probably poor or non-existent, giving no model to work from, and they may for years have found the entitlement unclear. In 1991 only 67 per cent of primary schools claimed to have a sex education policy (Thomson, 1992). However, with thorough preparation, team-work and support, feelings can be managed and progress made. The teachers' role is to advise governors on policy, then subsequently to put it into effect; to involve outside experts as appropriate; to keep abreast of suitable materials and approaches; to develop suitable procedures for implementing parents' rights of withdrawal; and to support parental provision of sex education at home if requested. Some teachers may for years have been competently delivering elements of sex education without having defined them as such, for example, developing self-esteem through 'circle time', or by teaching 'philosophy'. Here is a closer look at challenges teachers face.

Many nursery and primary school policies advocate that teachers answer questions about sex incidentally and spontaneously, particularly in early and infant years. As these responses are needs-led, internalisation is likely. The theory is fine, but what of difficulties in practice? A primary child cannot learn about sexual health without a working vocabulary which he or she can understand and use freely and interchangeably to communicate with peers, parents and teachers. In the opening to the controversial dictionary 'Sexwords' Jane Mills says:

> Most people at some time or other find themselves in a situation where they're talking about sex but can't confess they don't know the meaning of a certain word. Or they pretend to laugh at a rude joke, not daring to admit they don't have the slightest idea what's so funny. They then look the word up in the standard dictionary and get no help at all...
> (Mills, 1993)

Adults might be expected to have a wider vocabulary than children, and while they may not individually they certainly do collectively. A doctor may refer to 'down below', a cycling magazine to a woman's 'squishy bits', a biology text to her 'vulva' and 'vagina', friends to her fanny, Jack the lad to her 'cunt'. Moreover, she may be called a 'twat' and not realise that this is still the same thing although she does recognise it as an insult. A mum's medically described 'pregnancy' may appear in a biology text as the 'gestation of a foetus', and at home as 'having a baby'. However, words alone will not furnish children with sufficient information to understand what sexual health is. Somehow they need opportunities to make their own connections, and that is a critical part of the teacher's role.

A teacher describing a baby as coming out of its mummy's tummy (short for stomach) risks mixing it up with concepts of food. Internalised wrong or incomplete information is difficult to shift and could lead to potentially damaging misconceptions in adolescence as the following examples suggest:

● *'When mommy and daddy love each other very much they may have a baby.'*
Might this explain why some single teenage mothers give birth apparently without even realising that they could be pregnant having 'done it' once only to lose their virginity, without pleasure or love?

● *'Babies are made in bed when mummy and daddy lie very close together with their clothes off.'*

Research reveals two common misconceptions of adolescents are that you cannot get pregnant 'doing it' with your clothes on, or 'doing it' standing up. Your children take at face value all that is said to them.

Here is an interesting challenge for a teacher: can he or she easily find biologically correct non-slang words to explain unambiguously just what 'it' is that people so coyly 'do', and what possible connection it has with sexual health?

The National Survey of Sexual Attitudes and Lifestyles (Wellings, 1994) found that 20 per cent of women and 25 per cent of men aged under 24 years, claimed to have had their first experience of penetrative sex by the age of 16 years, though half said that they believed the experience had come too early, usually when inhibitions were weakened by peer-pressure, alcohol, and ignorance. Primary teachers can encourage sexual health indirectly by early teaching on other associated health issues, training pupils to be assertive (able to say 'no' and state clearly their personal preferences); by promoting abstinence both from early sexual intercourse and precocious alcohol use; and by encouraging more positively an alternative range of enjoyable activities, similarly perceived to reduce stress, and which contribute to a healthy adult lifestyle.

Meanwhile, research (Barnardos, 1992) indicates that children of eight and younger have heard enough about HIV/AIDS to worry them. They need reassurance and information on first aid, hygiene, keeping healthy, making friends with and caring for people who are HIV-positive, or who have developed AIDS and suffer increasing bouts of illness. Remember, transplant survivors too have an artificially suppressed immune system, to avoid 'rejection'. They and others with immune deficiency are prone to similar opportunistic diseases and need similar care.

An HIV-positive pupil presents a particular challenge. Does the child know of his or her condition? Has that child been emotionally damaged by people's possibly fearful reactions? Are all teachers told what is wrong with the child? What does he or she tell friends? What are the implications if the child crashes heads in the playground and both injured children have blood pouring down their faces as friends come to help them, apply initial first aid, and take them to find the duty teacher? In this case HIV could be passed on and eventually cause AIDS in its new host. Teachers as first aiders need to know and observe hygiene guidelines and agree policy on how to ensure that children maintain recommended standards of hygiene at all times in a matter of fact way, without developing fear. This approach eliminates the need to know who is HIV-positive, and prepares children to protect themselves in the unknown world of HIV outside school. A teacher's role is to keep up to date and model sensible approaches to HIV protection, for example by allowing pupils to see rubber gloves used and treated as an unremarkable part of daily hygiene routines (for official guidance see DES, 1991).

Peer-led education can support personal and social development of self-esteem, relationship skills, respect and a sense of responsibility. However, peers can also provide significant discontinuities in supporting each other's sexual health. Abused classmates may have precocious knowledge which they are more than willing to share inappropriately, in their efforts to come to terms with unwanted experiences. Anorexia is sometimes a response to sexual abuse, and anoretic females may have too low a height-weight ratio to sustain normal sexual development, delaying menarche. This raises two more implications for primary sex education. First, the need to establish clear child protection procedures, including training for classroom teachers to raise awareness of how to apply procedures if disclosure occurs; secondly, the need to teach healthy eating, backed up by congruent school dinner and tuckshop provision.

School managers seeking to maximise delivery of pupil entitlement and to minimise withdrawal of pupils by parents must devise a policy with which all feel comfortable and which teachers have the skills and motivation to implement. It is unsatisfactory to palm off 'sex education' on to student teachers during teaching practice. They may be young, unfamiliar with relevant law, unprepared by their course-work, and lacking breadth of knowledge in sexual matters. Entitlement is lost if time is allowed to slip past so that the end of term arrives before delivery is accomplished. Teachers as managers must be prepared to seek appropriate training, and to co-operate with other professionals such as the Health Promotion Officers of their Local Health Authority, local GPs and school nurses.

Conclusion

Press and media have great influence. The way they give constant attention to marriage breakup and family disturbance rather than affirming the security, commitment and love which is till the more widespread family experience is destabilising.

Perhaps the most sensitive and controversial issue teachers face is whose values to follow, and how differences can be negotiated to reach a resolution acceptable to the majority of parents, religious leaders and other community members in their catchment area.

In a health-promoting primary school a head teacher and assistant teachers each have the responsibility to be well-informed about a range of possible approaches, resources, and legislation concerning sex education. A number of publications (see bibliography) can help them advise governors and parents in the formulation of policy and practice. It is governors' responsibility to decide policy. Unmarried teachers with little personal sexual experience, and those in the midst of sexual trauma, may feel emotionally unready to contribute towards formal delivery. Their feelings should be respected. An effective referral system for child protection should be in place.

Spontaneous sharing of well-researched information across the curriculum allows teachers to match input to maturity, and sensitively to take into account each child's home experience. Additionally, a planned intervention in a regular timetabled lesson, or through topic work subject to normal testing and evaluation, will ensure that entitlement to knowledge, understanding, and skill development is not restricted by a child's own lack of knowledge of what to ask about; confidence to do the asking; or misunderstanding of answers provided.

First learning may be the only learning about sexual matters. Sexual health is best promoted by accuracy of vocabulary and information from the outset. It is important to work co-operatively. An optional pack for interested parents provided a month in advance of planned sex education to prepare for puberty would allow parents to share responsibility; prepare ahead with their child; reinforce classroom work; answer questions arising during the school programme; or enable them to provide effective alternative sex education themselves, supplemented by access to additional support materials, should they decide to opt their child out of the school programme.

Sex education is subject to OFSTED inspection:

To evaluate the quality of the school's programme for health education...it is likely inspectors will draw on evidence from the whole inspection team as the provision may be dispersed...(Handbook for the Inspection of Schools, Part 4.7.7b p74)

If adults take up the challenge to equip themselves appropriately, describe well the route to sexual health, take their children by the hand and lead them safely along it, then this is admirable and everyone will be a winner.

CHAPTER 6

Child Protection - Risk Reduction or Paranoia?

Eileen Bruce

> By listening to a single child we plant a sunflower seed. The long term effects could be truly magnificent.
>
> (Anne Bannister 1990)

Brief History and Past Legislation

Animals were protected sixty-seven years before legislation to protect children was introduced!

In the early 1820s, Mr Richard Martin MP took a donkey to court to press a charge of cruelty to the animal by its owner. Subsequently he introduced the first piece of animal welfare legislation. This was 'An Act to prevent the cruel and improper treatment of cattle'. (Moss 1961). Richard Martin became a founder of the RSPCA in 1824, and in that year sixty-three prosecutions for cruelty were brought to the courts, mostly from Smithfields Market.

No such similar legislation was available to protect children and the first prosecution for Child Protection was made under animal legislation.

More than one hundred years ago in Britain some efforts were being made to improve the treatment of children at work, for example in factories, mines and chimney sweeping, but these endeavours were set against a culture which, for economic reasons, appeared to accept the abuse of children. However, it is clear that there was an unwillingness to address the sensitive area of child abuse in the home by the introduction of legislation.

As late as 1880, Lord Shaftesbury, commenting on child abuse in the home, was quoted as saying, 'The evils are enormous and indisputable, but they are so private, internal and domestic a character as to be beyond the reach of legislation and the subject would not I think, be entertained in either House of Parliament.'

Events in America, however, led Lord Shaftesbury and others to re-address the needs of children and it is interesting to note that it was actually the RSPCA who helped to form the NSPCC in 1884.

> In 1884 the RSPCA helped to form the National Society For The Prevention of Cruelty to Children. In New York, Henry Bergh, pioneer of America's animal welfare societies, was asked to intercede on behalf of a little animal suffering at the hands of a woman. The little animal turned out to be a child. Bergh rose to the challenge and successfully prosecuted the woman for cruelty to an animal. After this many similar cases were brought and a special society was formed in New York to protect children. The RSPCA, informed of these events, decided that a similar organisation ought to be started in Britain and the necessary steps were taken by Lord Shaftesbury and the Rev. Benjamin Waugh.
>
> A Mr T.F. Agnew on his return to Liverpool reported the matter to Mr Samuel Smith, M.P. and Mr John Colam, and the RSPCA Committee did all they could to start a similar body in London. They commended the matter to the Lord Mayor of London, and at the Mansion House on 8th July 1884, Lord Shaftesbury moved, that it is desirable to form a London Society for the Prevention of Cruelty to Children. This was seconded, by Dr. Barnardo and supported by Cardinal Manning...and duly carried. (Turner 1964)

In 1886 the NSPCC was granted the use of the RSPCA boardroom at Jermyn Street for their meetings.

The first Charter for Children was eventually introduced in 1889. It was to be a further one hundred years before the passing of the Children Act 1989.

The Present Scene - Priority or Peripheral Education?

In a health-promoting primary school good practice has always included safety education, road safety, cycling proficiency, dangers in the home, at school and at play. In latter years 'Stranger Danger' has been a regular feature of the curriculum, with inputs from local police and community affairs officers. However, recent legislation, a rising tide of reported cases of concern, an acknowledgement of well documented tragedies (for example, Maria Colwell and the unacceptable horror disclosed in the Jamie Bulger murder trial) have alerted teachers to the need to expand programmes to encompass a personal dimension beyond those previously taught.

The need to consider this aspect of a young child's education raises many questions and uncertainties and rightly challenges our values and attitudes.

- Will we make the children frightened to talk to anyone they do not know?
- If 90 per cent of abusers are known to children how do we help them to differentiate between known adults?
- And what about children who abuse other children?
- How can I teach my health and sex education programme knowing I have a sexually abused child in the classroom?

- The very idea of abuse is abhorrent to me – how will I manage if a child discloses to me?
- Where do I stand legally if I refer a child and the case is unproven?
- There is always touching, comforting and hugging going on in primary classrooms – how do I stand now?
- What if the allegation is not proven – what of my relationships with parents then?

It is understandable and desirable that at a time when teachers are being asked not only to deliver the National Curriculum, with all the attendant pressures that this has brought, but are also required to be psychologists, social workers, police officers and parents for many children, they are questioning how much more they can be expected to deliver.

However, teachers are the ones who report suspected child abuse more frequently than other professions. They are very close to children, especially in the primary phase. The caring, observant and sensitive teacher is more able to detect changes in behaviour and demeanour.

Children frequently choose their teacher to disclose to. It is therefore essential that teachers respond with warmth, empathy and sensitivity, truly listening and believing. This is the greatest gift that children can receive at a time when they are often very confused and scared, feeling helpless and often believing that they are guilty.

The greatest publicity is usually accorded to sexual abuse but child abuse is much broader than that. Many facets of abuse are less easily acknowledged and are often more difficult to pursue. Child abuse encompasses physical, mental, social and emotional abuse together with neglect, racist and sexist abuse and all forms of bullying. There is a need to have a brief overview of recent legislation and the policies that are required pertaining to child abuse. It is essential that these are converted into positive and effective action in the classroom and the community. 'The Convention on the Rights of the Child adopted by the General Assembly of the United Nations', Unicef 1989, gives children the right to express their opinions and feelings and have these taken into account when decisions are made about their lives. It gives children an entitlement to be safe.

The most notable recent legislation has been the Children Act 1989 which came into force in England and Wales on 14 October 1991. It offers a coherent, systematic legal framework, encompassing nearly every aspect of the lives and upbringing of children.

Included in the Act is the requirement to protect children from harm by ensuring that all concerns about a child's safety are properly investigated in a way that causes the least distress and disruption to the child. It identifies schools as having a major preventative role.

'Working Together Under the Children Act 1989', HMSO 1991, offers guidance to schools on adopting policies and procedures when abuse is disclosed but also guidance on preventative strategies in the curriculum. It also includes a section (5.24) on 'Abuse carried out by children and young people'. It stresses the need to 'ensure that such behaviour is treated seriously' and that appropriate child protection procedures should be followed in respect of both the victim and the alleged abuser. This has clear implications for bullying incidents in particular.

The Elton Report (1989) which addressed discipline in schools states 'a sense of community cannot be achieved if a school does not take seriously bad behaviour which mainly affects pupils rather than teachers.'

The Health of the Nation, (DOH 1990), contains recommendations with implications for this area of the curriculum, in particular, its targets pertaining to Mental Health and HIV and AIDS. The DFE Circular on Sex Education in Schools (DFE 5/94), replacing Circular 11/87, allows parents the right, from 1 September 1994, to withdraw their children from all or part of sex education, except for those areas covered by programmes of study in the National Curriculum. This withdrawal, if chosen, could have grave implications for some children's development, safety and well-being, as it will be quite difficult to address some aspects of personal safety without reference to sexual development.

National Curriculum Guidance 5 Health Education (1990) includes modules on safety, family life, sex education and psychological health. At Key Stage 1 the Sex Education component outlines expectations that pupils will 'know about personal safety, e.g. know that individuals have rights over their own bodies and that there are differences between good and bad touches; begin to develop simple skills and practices which will help maintain personal safety'.

Whole School Policies in a Health-Promoting School

These take time – a most precious commodity – commitment to the task and energy and enthusiasm to see them through. However, the rewards can be immense and eventually save time and produce a quality response *if* the policy is translated into practice with its efficacy monitored and amended when necessary.

The relevant policies with implications for child protection are those required and identified in the OFSTED *Handbook for the Inspection of Schools* (1993), namely:

a) Behaviour
b) Sex Education
c) Personal, Social and Health Education
d) Health and Welfare
e) Child Protection
f) Bullying – which can be part of Behaviour or Child Protection Policy.

The construction of policies should involve a corporate response and not, as frequently happens, one teacher being told 'write a policy for...' and then being given a totally unrealistic time scale for completion. The 'policy' is often then the idiosyncratic view of one very overworked but conscientious individual. Inevitably, such a policy cannot take account of a range of views and expertise.

A working party with a very clear focus and time scale and clearly identified tasks can develop productive partnerships with a range of people who have much to offer. These may include pupils, parents, governors, police, church representatives, lunchtime supervisors, teachers, school nurse, education welfare officers, educational psychologists, caretakers and school secretaries. Such a group can enhance working relationships across a whole range of other areas and contributions from pupils can often be quite inspiring and salutary! Communicating and negotiating in this way can provide consistency and continuity and avoid conflict, confrontations and coercion.

Laying Foundations for Good Practice

What do we mean by this frequently used term, 'school ethos'? When is a school 'health-promoting'? What particular relevance do these terms have for child protection? Ethos has an almost metaphysical feel to it, a 'wil o' the wisp' texture, difficult to define – but it can be experienced the moment schools are entered. It is about the immediate evidence of courtesy, care and respect that is accorded to everyone in school, be they children, staff or the whole school team and its visitors. Reception by the school secretary can be so welcoming, regardless of the piles of dinner money just counted for the third time, the child who is about to vomit, and the delivery of stationery that has just arrived and blocked the hallway! There is a distinct feeling that people value each other, children's names are known and they know the expectations the school family shares. Staff rooms are welcoming and the atmosphere is supportive to colleagues – even when the photocopier has broken down for the third time in as many days!

In spite of the stress and pace of the school day, people listen to each other, they have put co-operative working relationships high on their own agendas and hold self-esteem and positive self-image to be their core curriculum for children and adults. It may sound like an unachievable goal but it does need at least to be at a 'working towards' level for effective child protection to take place.

It is much easier to achieve set goals if expectations are explored with parents when children are first registered for school. Many schools have already drawn up codes of conduct expected from children and the support parents will be required to give. More than anything else parents want children to be happy and safe in school.

Entry behaviour of children is an enormous variable and very, very often unacceptable behaviour has to be unlearnt. The major complaints from lunchtime supervisors are about the behavioural aspects of the children – 'they swear, kick, punch and bully' or 'they are much worse than they used to be, much more violent and aggressive'. It is interesting to note also that many lunchtime supervisors have been in post for many years and have received no training in managing behaviour of children. Yet they are in charge of often four times as many children as teachers are asked to teach in a controlled situation.

If a child is going to spend one fifth of its school life in the playgrounds, and have approximately 1300 playtimes during its school days, then surely this is an area where they will learn, and practise, personal and social skills? Should we not then be providing an effective training programme for supervisors? In many schools children are unmanageable after their playground encounters, especially during the lunchtime. 'Policing' play does not help them to develop. (See Wright, D. Chapter 7.)

Play has been perceived as a natural part of childhood but it is becoming increasingly evident that many children have never learnt how to play. On a positive note, many Health Visitors are liaising with teachers to work out ways of helping parents to work and play with their children. This may then make school an exciting and fulfilling experience for new arrivals, rather than a battleground that perpetuates the 'bash 'em back' principle. Children are twice as likely to be bullied in primary schools. They are most vulnerable after starting school at five or six years and on moving school at around 11 or 12 years.

Child abuse, including bullying, is a totally classless phenomenon and children from all social environments need the opportunity to experience a positive preventative programme. However, it should never be a 'bolt-on' activity. It must be embedded in a school that has already recognised that its own ethos will be an integral part of the education process.

The health-promoting school is many faceted and includes health concerns such as availability of hot water and soap in the toilets, a litter free environment and attention to good hygiene practices in the dining room. However, at the heart of a health-promoting school are relationships. It is acknowledged that children are entitled to opportunities for developing self-empowerment; to a recognition of their need to have a sense of their own value, to be loved and to be safe and in preventative terms a chance to practise skills and acquire knowledge in a well prepared and planned curriculum.

If teachers and other educators are to carry out a preventative programme of child protection it is obviously desirable to have a training opportunity to explore their own values and to become familiar with child protection procedures. There is also a need to have 'hands on' experience of the many resources available and to consider active participative teaching strategies to use with the children.

It is always possible that this work may generate a disclosure from a child and even from a teacher. Support structures must be in place for both of them. Although a designated teacher is required to be trained in child protection procedures, and in many schools they are the only ones who have been trained, opportunities should be seized for *all* teachers, support staff and governors to avail themselves of preparatory training before a situation arises. A health-promoting primary school will provide this opportunity!

Practical Strategies in the Classroom

'Prevention is better than cure' – than having to respond to a disclosure – and the primary curriculum is an opportunity to try to 'turn off the tap' instead of 'mopping up the flood'. Many teachers are already undertaking a considerable amount of first class teaching which lends itself to developing preventative strategies in child protection. However, this may be acknowledged and recorded under other headings, for example, safety or relationships.

- What are the key components in a safety programme?
- What are some of the issues we need to take into account?
- What are the needs of children in the primary phase?

Key components

These must include elements which address:

a) the development of positive self-esteem, self-image and self-awareness;
b) knowledge that is age-appropriate and which is revisited and reinforced at regular intervals;
c) facilities for practising skills of decision-making, problem-solving and assertiveness;
d) strategies for dealing with threatening situations;
e) opportunities to explore different feelings, the nature of friendship and of families;
f) how to manage anger and conflict;
g) how to resist negative peer pressure and adult persuasion;
h) respecting self and others;
i) understanding codes of conduct and class ground rules;
j) trusted adults and support networks;
k) rules designed for safety;
l) fun;
m) learning to listen;
n) for teacher the need to follow agreed procedures of the school and LEA where appropriate;
o) how to use positive peer group pressure.

Key issues to consider

a) Language capacity and limitations ("I was raped" – 'raped' may be the only descriptive word known).
b) Children with special needs and/or learning difficulties. Recognise that these children are very vulnerable.
c) Make sure you do not teach this as a problem but as a challenge.
d) Keeping good relationships with parents is very desirable but never lose sight of the fact that the well-being of a child is paramount.
e) The confused messages children receive through the media.
f) Recognise that children from different cultures and beliefs may have different behaviour patterns.
g) Some children may enjoy 'inappropriate' hugs and touches because it

addresses a need for love, warmth and affection that is denied them elsewhere.

h) Are there children in the lessons who you know have been abused? Have you planned to be sensitive to this without denying the others a preventative programme?

i) Do we by our own teaching style occasionally abuse children? 'We never had this behaviour from your brother'! 'You idiot!' 'Cloth ears!'

j) Confidentiality – there are different guide-lines for different professions. This can cause difficulty – enquire as a matter of interest!

k) Have you very strong feelings about child abuse? How are you going to address/confront these?

In a health-promoting primary school the child protection theme should be woven like threads into the fabric of the curriculum without any noticeable seams... It should be a magical journey to be shared with children, exploring new pathways and experiences, reading signs that might mean danger but giving the explorers the journey's end safely. The learning process will have implications for the broadest development of positive well-being and potential for children well beyond child protection issues.

The Nursery and Early Years

Most of what I really need to know about how to live and what to do, and how to be I learned at nursery school. Wisdom was not at the top of the university mountain, but there in the sand pit. These are things I learned. Share everything. Play fair. Don't hit people. Put things back where you found them. Clean up your own mess. Don't take things that aren't yours. Say you're sorry when you hurt somebody. Wash your hands before you eat. Live a balanced life. Learn a bit and think a bit, and draw and sing and dance and play and work every day.

Take a nap in the afternoon, When you go out into the world, watch for traffic, hold hands and stick together. Be aware of wonder. Remember the little seed in the plastic cup. The roots go down and the plant goes up, and nobody really knows why, but we are all like that.

Goldfish and hamsters and white mice and even the little seed in the plastic cup – they all die. So do we.

And then remember one of the first words you learned to read, the biggest word of all: look. Think what a better world it would be if we all had biscuits and milk about three o'clock every afternoon and then lay down with our blankets for a nap. Or if we had a basic policy always to put things back where we found them and cleaned up our own messes. And it is still true, no matter how old you are, when you go out into the world, it is best to hold hands and stick together. (Robert Fulgnum)

The vital early years of children's education and development should include opportunities to develop skills and practices to maintain their personal safety. Programmes in personal and social skills can help to map the beginning of our journey.

It is hoped the following will be an affirmation of current good practice.

A mix of age-appropriate materials and methods should be used, with each input being of a short duration and being re-visited and extended at fairly regular intervals to accommodate limited concentration spans and recall.

Suggested methodologies for the Nursery and Early Years

1 Stories and poems (children's library useful source)
2 Answering questions honestly
3 Posing questions to initiate problem-solving, decision-making
4 Using media events
5 Using puppets
6 Picture making using a wide variety of materials/also collages
7 Writing poems/stories
8 Using tape recordings
9 Drama and role-play/dressing up
10 Using photographs
11 Using soft, cuddly toys
12 Appropriate videos
13 Variety of artwork
14 Movement, dance and PE
15 Activities to enhance self-esteem

Ever-increasing numbers of resources are available offering excellent planning guides that take account of differing levels of concepts, knowledge and skills, issues of continuity, progression and differentiation with endless lesson plans and activities.

The five resources that follow have been used by the author throughout the primary phase and they have been sound foundations for Personal, Social and Health Education programmes. They offer accessible and user-friendly ideas for busy classroom practitioners, including a wealth of ideas for promoting the protection of children.

1 *Skills for the Primary School Child* – Promoting the protection of children Parts 1 and 2, TACADE
2 *Health for Life* Books 1 and 2
3 *Child Protection – A whole school curriculum approach* – Inset Resources and Teaching Resources Gill Evans (Avon)
4 *Turn Your School Around* Jenny Mosley
5 *Kidscape* materials, including 'A Programme for Prevention of Sexual Assault on Children' Michele Elliott

A sample selection of ideas for classroom activities in the Early Years

Circle Time - Listening skills and taking turns

Purpose
A fun way of learning to take turns; the beginning of accepting rules; learning to respect the rights of others; sharing and working as a group; being heard (often a shy or introverted child will speak with more confidence once they have the comfort of the 'frog'); communication and language development; expressing worrying and scary thoughts when other ways are difficult; finding out others have the same interests, feelings, fears as you do.

Resource
A small toy, e.g. a frog

Activity
Only the holder of the frog can speak, everyone else must listen. If the frog is passed or thrown to someone who does not want to speak they can pass it on.
Make the task VERY SIMPLE AND VERY SHORT, e.g. "Stroke the frog and tell us about..." (choose one of the following):
  a) your favourite toy;
  b) one thing you are good at;
  c) one thing that makes you happy;
  d) one thing that makes you scared;
  e) what gives you a 'good' feeling or a 'bad' feeling.

Notes
Motor skills and behaviour patterns need to be considered. A frog full of tiny beads (well sealed) the floppier the better, is very popular. Try gift and toy shops?

Feeling Good About Me

Purpose
To begin to develop an understanding of the uniqueness of self and an appreciation of own capabilities and achievements; developing self-esteem; and appreciating the qualities of others.

Resources
A drawing of a tall tree – draw just a trunk and bare branches that can be fixed to the back of a door or on a wall; a large quantity of leaves cut out of green sugar paper; glue sticks or Blu-Tack.

Activity
Put out small piles of leaves. Ask the children to write one thing they are good at in the middle of a leaf and put it on one of the branches of the tree. Give an example. Teacher to put her or his leaf on tree.

Extension
Write one thing on a leaf that is good about another child in the class.

Notes
The tree becomes 'beautiful' very quickly with positive and visual acknowledgement of the good things each child contributes. They can add to the tree at any time and they do – blossom, birds, animals. (NB If you use the leaves to acknowledge good qualities in others, make sure no child is left out!)

Variations
Friendship trees (Friendly Deeds) and Mobiles
Creating flower garden (Qualities/good deeds on petals)
Recipes for a friend, including ingredients and methods
Highly recommended – *Skills for the Primary School Child* TACADE, and *Self-Esteem – A Classroom Affair* Volumes 1 and 2, Michele and Craig Borba – An essential purchase.

Good touches, Bad touches

Purpose
To experience good and bad feelings in a safe environment and to learn how to manage these situations and one's feelings.

Resources
'Feely bags' containing a variety of small items of different shapes and textures.

Activity
Working in pairs, children tell partners what item they feel in the bag, whether they like it/dislike it and how it makes them feel. Take items out of bag. Do all children like/dislike the same things?
Record by children drawing round their left hand. Along the fingers write the things their hands like to touch. Repeat with the right hand and along the fingers write the things they hate to touch.

Extension
Make a frieze of the hands, write poems, lists of things that hands are good for (e.g. artists, nurses, comforting) and bad for (e.g. stealing, hitting, breaking things).
   Children draw a picture of their body. Colour in green all the parts they do not mind being touched and colour red all the parts they hate being touched.

Private parts in public places

Draw a picture of your body, then draw some clothes on your own special private parts that you keep covered in public places, e.g. swimming baths, on the beach, doing PE.

Who are the only people we let touch our special places (e.g. doctors, nurses, mum, dad)? Discuss.

Excellent materials in *Child Protection – A Whole Curriculum Approach* Gill Evans (Avon) and *Kidscape* materials.

Problem-solving

Purpose
Exploring skills of problem-solving in a variety of situations; learning coping skills and strategies when they might be alone; developing skills in valuing, summarising, discussing and reviewing.

Resources
Photographs, media reports, different relevant scenarios.
Especially useful *Interaction - A Teachers' Resource Book* Level 3 and *Interaction – Picture Resources Chart*. Activity 16. Also *Think Bubble* video (9.5 minutes), audio cassette and Teaching Notes (Home Office) for 4-7 year age group.

Activity
Show photographs of situations to the group and ask for suggestions to solve the problems. (If individual photographs are used these can be issued to small groups.)
Example situations can include:
1 you are alone in the house and someone knocks the door;
2 you have lost your front door key and there is no one in;
3 you are approached by a man in the park who invites you to see some newly hatched birds in a nest in the bushes;
4 you have fallen over and a stranger offers to help you.

Record responses in words and pictures. Make a 'Safe house/safe environment' corner using children's work.

Notes
Use these activities to include how to say no FIRMLY, politely but assertively.

Some sample ideas for the Junior Years

It is important that previous work is built on and extended, and the resources already recommended for the Early Years have excellent materials for continuity in the later years in the primary phase.

What's inside? – Developed from My Body Project

Purpose
To develop an understanding of how the body is made and the wonder of its workings. How it protects us and how we can protect it.

Resources
Rolls of wallpaper (very cheap odd rolls from decorator shops), felt pens.
Model skeleton (borrow from LEA or Health Promotion Department).
Model torso (borrow from LEA's or Health Promotion Departments).
The Human Body slides, posters and Teaching Notes (Philip Green series).

Activity
Lie a child on a length of wallpaper. Draw round the body. When completed the empty outline is filled in by a group of children working together. From prior knowledge fill in the organs in the right places, about the right size and colour. Name the parts. Display when completed. Groups talk about the body they have created – several groups can do this activity at the same time and report back. When all 'bodies' are completed bring out the torso and skeleton and check results!

Extension
   a) What does each of the body parts do?
   b) What are the different systems of the body?
   c) Which parts of the body protect other parts, e.g. skull protects brain, ribs protect lungs, heart; skin protects the whole, keeping organs in and the swimming baths and germs out!
   d) Protective clothing (and private parts in public places), protect from sun, cold, view.
   e) Good food protects from illness.
   f) Good hygiene protects from germs and smells.
   g) Immunisation/vaccination protects from serious illnesses.
   h) Sensible behaviour protects from ill-health (no smoking).
   i) Sensible behaviour – not taking risks – helps keep our body safe.
   j) Growing up and body changes and need for care and protection.

Notes
This is an effective activity, starting 'where the child is at' it can lead into sex education and the child's rights over his or her own body, and personal responsibility. It allows children who find writing and reading difficult to contribute, and to succeed – self-esteem, language and communication flow unimpeded. This is also an excellent activity with parents on a Parents Evening, as long as the floor is carpeted! The activity has a huge fun element for children as well as being challenging and appropriate.

Lesson Cards from Skills for the Primary School Child, TACADE

There are so many relevant lesson plans in this pack it is almost impossible to select material. However, at the junior stage the following examples illustrate recommended areas for development (a very useful adjunct is the way they are related to the National Curriculum Attainment Targets):

1 Section 3.3 Solving conflicts peacefully
2 Section 4.3 Learning to negotiate
3 Section 4.4 Being assertive
4 Section 5.2 Taking risks
5 Section 5.3 Pressure and influences
6 Section 5.4 Being responsible
7 Section 5.5 Supporting each other
8 Section 6.3 When is a secret not a secret?
9 Section 6.4 Safe people, safe places, safe things

These materials are very user-friendly for those who have never undertaken this work before. They also allow plenty of opportunity for using individual professional expertise and personal ideas.

Bullying

Bullying is not always perceived to be a facet of child abuse but that is exactly what it is. In fact, if some of the violence which occurs in our schools occurred out in the community it could constitute grievous bodily harm or intimidation. (See Wright, D. Chapter 7)

The health-promoting primary school provides an environment where it is clearly understood that bullying will not be tolerated, that it is a 'telling school' where there are basic ground rules and expectations which are there to enable children to be safe and happy. Research indicates that bullying behaviour must be addressed before a child reaches the age of eight for intervention to be effective, so those old adages of 'he'll grow out of it' or 'she is just going through a phase' are not necessarily true, particularly if the behaviour occurs repeatedly and wilfully.

Bullying has rightly attained a much higher profile in the last two years and many different approaches have been used to address the problem. Close encounters of the bullying kind, from working with the troubled child to sharing the aftermath of suicide (the most recent being eleven years old), have highlighted some key components that repeatedly appear when improved and successful procedures and programmes have been tried.

These include:
- A whole school policy that includes bullying (often included in Behaviour and Child Protection Policies) formulated as described earlier in this chapter, using contributions from a wide variety of people.
- All new parents are given a school booklet containing a clear policy statement about acceptable and expected behaviour, sanctions and what to do if they are worried.
- Parents may be asked to sign the school conduct code, agreeing to support it (but they cannot legally be made to do this).

- Pupils sign the school policy statement about behaviour and code of practice, if this is possible.
- In-service training about the management of behaviour is available for all staff including support staff.
- Playtimes (including wet days) are adequately supervised, with the provision of adequate and varied activities which provide a stimulus for positive play and social interaction. If necessary, stagger the starting and finishing times of play.
- Sanctions and penalties are agreed and clearly understood by everyone.
- The health-promoting primary school is a 'telling school' and it is known that designated members of staff will always listen and deal with a situation.

There are many approaches in vogue for managing bullying incidents. It is always essential to listen to the victim and also to the bully and to record serious incidents in children's files. For children who can write it is useful for all those involved to write down what occurred, and to bring them face to face with the aim of talking it through, understanding the feelings involved and encouraging an apology. In incidents of a serious nature, it is important to ask the respective parents to come to school to facilitate a resolution. This is infinitely better than parents tackling the incident outside school, for bad feelings can continue long after the children have put the incident behind them. In very serious cases it may be advisable to call for police intervention. Suspending a child should always be the last resort but where circumstances are extreme and all else fails it may be necessary. Regrettably, suspension is no longer a necessary option only in secondary schools, as the level of violence in primary schools has escalated in recent years.

The 'No Blame Approach' is a method of management which has received much publicity and acclaim. The philosophy of this method is to bring together the bully/bullies, the victim and any colluders/bystanders/observers. The idea is to develop empathy between them and collectively to put together strategies to improve or resolve the bullying situations.

Concern about this approach is, largely, that retribution and justice is not so clearly seen by others (including parents) to be carried out in the usually accepted manner. The crucial issue is to have a whole school policy in place, to which everyone has contributed in order to be understood by all.

The ideas outlined earlier in this chapter can be used as a foundation for a safety programme which includes bullying. It can be complemented by a range of activities, including assemblies, drama and role-play, 'What if' questions, art projects/poster designs/photographic and video work, stories and poems and assertiveness training.

Conclusion

It is an inescapable reality that child abuse pervades the life experiences of many children. Entitlement to child protection is an essential part of a health-promoting primary school. It should provide the ideal environment within which a truly effective contribution to the protection of children from all forms of abuse can be made.

The determinants of successful practice will be: the ethos of the school with its caring and respecting relationships; strong partnerships with parents and the community; healthy alliances with supporting agencies, but above all the determination, motivation and commitment to treasure each and every child, to empower them to succeed, to value themselves and to develop protective skills to keep them safe from harm.

An Ancient Chinese Proverb states, 'A child's life is like a piece of paper on which every passer-by leaves a mark'.

Indelible marks of healthy, positive life experiences should be every child's entitlement, created by trusted, empathetic adults who can help prevent or erase traumatic events. This is the birthright of every single child.

CHAPTER 7

All Together Now - Towards a Whole School Behaviour Policy

David Wright

Introduction: From Myth to Methodology

> 'The trouble all started,' muttered a harassed infant teacher, 'when we allowed children to get out of their seats.'

Spend a day in any school staff-room in Britain and the odds are that the bad behaviour of the children will be a topic for discussion at some point. 'Discussion' may be too grand a word for the exasperated soundbites between sips of strong coffee, and many would be better not recorded. Younger members of staff might bemoan their own inability to keep a particular child on task for more than one minute. They might be supplied with ingenious solutions by middle-rankers which, if carried through, would result in teacher exclusion *sine die* or – much worse – exposure by the tabloid press.

'Tying children to their chairs' was a solution recommended in the 1810 edition of *The British System of Education* (Lancaster 1810), but that might raise a few eyebrows today – even at the DFE. Older members of staff may not remember so far back, but will still point to a 'golden age' when the teacher's word was law and parental involvement meant dad giving his offspring a good thrashing if the school as much as reported a misdemeanour. Reference to old school log books and punishment books will lay the myth of any halcyon era. 'Writing on the wall', 'repeated talking', 'interference with the electric lights', 'molesting neighbours' and 'throwing water about the lobby' are common entries. More serious offences – 'knife throwing', 'setting fire to an empty cellar' and 'indecent assault' (for which one culprit received 'a sound flogging') figure less frequently, but with a regularity that would alarm today. An entry from 1929 – 'Bullying small boys by taking cigarette cards from them before being allowed to drink' – and a punishment of 'four on the seat' suggests an awareness of – and response to – a current 'problem' (Birmingham School Board Punishment Book - Benson Road School, 1929). In the same book, concurrent entries for 1934 point to an inconsistency and subjectivity apparent today in teacher response. Poor 'Norman Pitts' received two strokes for 'opening the teacher's desk', yet 'Harry Harlow' received only one stroke for 'using the drinking fountain as a urinal'. (Sorry if you're still around, Norman and Harry, but it is a matter of public record – and interest!) In retrospect, the four strokes for the cigarette card extortionist seems harsh in view of the public service they were providing by dissuading children from using the fountain.

Rough analyses as to the causes of inappropriate behaviour were no doubt as common in bygone staffrooms as they are today. Changes in learning and teaching styles, alluded to by the infant teacher above, may have been a recurring theme. Perhaps our present disquiet about the detrimental effects of television and video games echoes concerns expressed with the advent of 'popular' radio. Similarly, we might be able to relate the consumption of 'junk' food to the malnutrition of the 1930s; the example set by present 'public' figures with the abdication of Edward VIII and the abolition of capital and corporal punishment with a decline in the option of transportation for life.

There is more than a grain of truth running through such 'common' sense. Teachers *know* what they experience. Even teachers with a few years' experience are able to give evidence of increased levels of disruption. They will also attest to increasing pressures and responsibilities as a result of rapid implementation of the 1988 Education Reform Act (HMSO,1988). Perhaps the point at issue is whether there has been a real decline in standards of discipline and an increase in the number of children displaying inappropriate behaviour, or whether, particularly over the last decade, there has been a diminishing capacity of schools to cope with what has always been a constant problem. Clear evidence is emerging that, whilst the latter may be true, the level of indiscipline is increasing. Another question to ask is whether this perceived increase will 'peak' and then decline with, as some suggest, a return to better social and economic conditions.

One thing is certain: 'significant' inappropriate behaviour will not go away in the lifetime of even today's youngest teacher. That must be faced. The masters and mistresses who came before us coped in their time and in their way, endeavouring, with success, to improve the lot of children. History can inform: that is its strength. We must not allow it to be mere fables of an earlier 'Utopia', in which to take refuge. Staffroom moans and groans and light-hearted 'barrack room' analyses are essential to maintain sanity, but they must not become destructive. For a start, would it not be better for us all to see the inappropriate behaviour of our children as a challenge rather than a problem? Negative attitudes of staff are readily recognised and reflected by children. In the context of the health-promoting primary school, it would be a good start if we thought of ourselves as continually being challenged rather than continually having problems.

That is not to say that teachers' intimate perspectives should not be voiced at all political levels. This very point emphasises that the challenges we face must be seen and responded to in group terms, whether that group be the whole class, the whole staff, the whole community or the whole nation. A teacher has not failed if she or he cannot control the class; it is the whole school, the community, the 'powers that be' who have failed to support the teacher. Apportioning blame to the children themselves, the parents, the previous class teacher, ineffective senior management, the lack of psychological support or local and national politicians is not productive – however blameworthy they may be. How much better if all work together to achieve success, realising our own and others' strengths and weaknesses and building upon what we can do well together. Unity is strength; strength of which we can all feel a part, providing a boost to morale which, in turn, sustains and develops both mental and physical well-being. Also, the joy – and therapy – in admitting our own failings is in the realisation that many share them. Healthy criticism provides a necessary analysis upon which to develop the group and the individual. By the same token, group members will often identify and reinforce a particular strength of an individual – one that the individual has been too modest to admit. It is the drive towards a common purpose, with common aims and ideals, and a commitment to *all* children, which builds team-work. We must rise above any political climate which negates, say, co-operation in favour of competition. We need to build structures in which all are encouraged.

Such structures protect, comfort and calm all within. Teachers, ancillaries and children need to go home at the weekend with enough mental and physical reserve to recover rapidly over the Friday evening, enjoy their weekend 'free time' and return, fresh for the challenge of another week.

Children Behave ...in spite of ...

The reasons for the ways in which we all choose to behave or not to behave are equally varied and complex and turn upon themselves. This is not the place to enter too deeply the realms of academia. Such intellectual pursuits have provided valuable insights, particularly when supported by scientifically conducted observations, and a knowledge of them is essential bag and baggage for the aspiring teacher. However, they may not serve the purpose of a nursery teacher who needs a quick remedy for a child presently throwing tantrums in the middle of the classroom. Neither will it help the Year 6 teacher whose class of thirty-five will never line up properly at playtime. We need to know what it is that makes children behave well with us, and amongst themselves, in the here and now.

We hear much of the socio-economic factors which inhibit a child's healthy development (Townsend and Davidson, 1982; Whitehead, 1988). They are very real and need to be addressed at all levels from the personal to the political. But it helps little to know that 'Jenny' has a troubled family history when we are trying to dissuade her from battering the child next to her for 'looking at her'. Knowledge of what has worked with Jenny to defuse recent classroom crises are more practical. That is not to say that knowledge of 'background' or special factors is not important to a teacher or counsellor. It is essential for a sympathetic, understanding approach in the developing relationship between teacher and child. It might be an appeal to that relationship which of itself encourages a 'Jenny' to desist in violence. What must be avoided is the attitude expressed with – "What do you expect with his/her background?". We are doing children no favours if we do not encourage them to respond appropriately in a variety of contexts, no matter what inadequacies we might *believe* there have been in their social development as a result of poor housing, poor parenting, unsatisfactory schooling or the multitude of other factors which may stifle potential. Stereotyping by race, colour, class or creed blinkers the viewer and not only prevents a breadth and richness in the teacher's own understanding but, quite unfairly, restricts opportunity for those viewed.

This is not to say we must not recognise the very real pressures that children and parents suffer as a result of social and economic injustice. Parents who are having to work unsocial hours in order just to feed the family might not be able to attend the one and only parents' evening. Any criticism or condemnation of them – and their child by association – for lack of interest could be unfounded. Flexible arrangements for parent/teacher meetings would be an obvious answer. Similarly, many white, British teachers may be unaware of the depth of feeling and anguish amongst ethnic minorities in respect of the pervasive racism within society. The 1993 Asylum and Immigration Appeals Act (HMSO,1993) may be viewed dispassionately by some in Britain, but to Black Britons of all ages, even the very young, it gives a clear message of rejection. The protestations of government that the legislation is not racist in nature carry little weight with Britons of Caribbean and Asian origin who perceive those clauses which provide for arbitrary refusal without appeal as open to discrimination. Their misgivings are founded upon a knowledge and experience of prior immigration policy and practice (MacDonald 1991).

Given the host of trials and tribulations that many children suffer, it is a wonder that they can give as much as they do in their relationships with adults and peers. For that we should be thankful.

Children Behave Because They Trust Us

Children have great hopes for the future and trust that we as teachers, parents or carers share, and are promoting, their aspirations. Have you, for example, ever poured scorn on any nine year old who has just announced that he or she is going to be a professional footballer when you 'know' that he or she has two left feet and is the last person to be picked at the playing fields? What is your reaction to the eleven year old whose parents have entered their son or daughter for the 'grammar' school selection tests when your records show a reading age of just over six? Your heart may sink, but you do nothing to diminish their hopes. You protect them by responding positively and with no little skill – "That's good, Nigel, but you will have to work hard, and don't be disappointed if you don't get a place". It's a lot better than "You haven't got a cat in hell's chance". They feel secure in the knowledge that we are working to provide them with the where-withal to succeed. This might not be apparent to us. We all know of the many children who will not put pen to paper without the threat of eternal missed play-times and they themselves may not be conscious that they are putting their trust in us... For children, all adults (whether teachers, parents, police officers or the local crossing warden) retain an aura of knowledge and experience. If you doubt this, the downside of such trust is the level of unrecorded sex abuse. Children trust that what we are doing to them is generally all right. There *are* times when they think you are being totally unfair. The very small child may bawl its head off if it can't have a bag of sweets; some fourteen year olds can feel aggrieved if parents do not allow them to stay out until 2 a.m. at the local disco, and we have all experienced a junior child publicly refusing to finish a piece of 'necessary' work. In a backhanded way they are probably emphasising that trust. With you they can feel secure in letting it all go.

It has often been stated that children have a keen sense of what is fair. Whilst an individual might readily accept the sanction of two missed playtimes, he or she would be extremely upset if another child received only one missed playtime for the same offence. Similarly, rewards for similar achievement must be equi-table if you are to avoid a classroom riot and the vilification and scorn of those who 'unfairly' receive the most by those who receive the least. The parable of 'The workers in the Vineyard' – where half-day workers received the same pay as full-day workers – does not go down too well with Year 5. Again, they trust that you will get it right, hence the over-reaction when you do not. Any breach of trust, any blatant unfairness, will be long remembered. A child who has been sanctioned because the parent had not been able to send in the school dinner money will have little regard for the applier of the sanction, will be difficult to handle from then on, and may hold a lifelong grudge. This point emphasises the need for teachers and parents to be aware of the demands and difficulties each experience. A working partnership between parents and teachers can help to ensure that children do not suffer from possible contradictory priorities of home and school (TACADE, 1990).

Children Behave If They Are Interested In What They Are Doing

There is much merit in the belief that a relevant and interesting curriculum is the answer to inappropriate behaviour. To broaden that, children will be no problem to you if they are actively engaged on a task. In the national 'adult' context, ris-ing levels of unemployment have been accompanied by rising levels of crime – although the correlation is not so simplistic and requires deeper analysis (Gow *et al.*, 1989). As teachers, we have a greater opportunity to control and manage our own micro situation and to ensure stimulating environments which provide for positive activity. It is as much the right of children to have such environments as to be properly fed.

However, no matter how positive your environment, how varied your activities, how integrated your style and how brilliant and charismatic a teacher you are, the children in your care will 'misbehave'. They are human. There would be a greater concern about children – and teacher – if they did not. There are, of course, varying degrees of misbehaviour. Serious incidents are rare, but more reportable. The findings from the *National Survey of Teachers in England and Wales* (Gray and Sime, 1988, reported in Appendix D of the Elton Report *Disruption in Schools* HMSO,1989) clearly demonstrated that it was common, low-level disruption such as talking out of turn and hindering other pupils that annoyed most teachers. There are children whose levels of concentration are minimal. They become easily bored and often 'discover' negative ways of applying your most positively arranged activities or, worse still, wander about other groups provoking discontent. There are even children who will actively seek ways to disturb and disrupt from the outset. Good classroom management – thoughtful, well planned and well prepared lessons in surroundings conducive to learning – will keep most of the children, and you, happy most of the time. The cutting edge of behaviour management has to do with what you do when the levels of disruption or inappropriate behaviour, partly outlined above, are such as to impede the learning process. You have a need to teach and the children need to learn. Frustration is apparent when those needs are not met. It is necessary for all those concerned with the educative process to develop a behavioural structure that will assist that process.

Children Behave If They Are Involved In The Process

A behaviour audit can provide a wealth of information about practices and attitudes and opinions in respect of the current behaviour policy – or lack of it! Children have intimate knowledge of what is going on in school and what concerns them most. They are the ones for whom the policy is being designed. It seems obvious that they should be involved from the start. Pupil questionnaires and/or class discussions quickly identify areas of concern. 'Bullying' is a classic reply, but others have included 'being continually hit by the footballs', 'people stealing my crisps' and even 'being disturbed whilst trying to work'! It is interesting to note that 'bullying' became a high profile issue as a result of children being listened to and their concerns taken seriously. What affects children in *their* world might not be as apparent or significant to adults who, with the best of intentions, sometimes identify and prescribe for them.

Confidential, unsigned questionnaires can determine the level of violence. Questions such as 'How many times have you hit/kicked someone this week and why?' have also provided revealing statistics.

Even the very young can participate. They might not be able to complete a questionnaire, but they can be interviewed by older juniors.

Children can also be 'agents' in widening the audit. Schools may develop parent questionnaires which can be carried home by the children. The problem of returning the completed questionnaires can easily be solved by giving a team point to those children who bring them back.

At an adult level there is a need for senior management leadership and guidance, both to initiate parts of the process, as above, and also to involve all sections of the school community. Meetings might be arranged for individual groups (teachers, lunchtime supervisors, governors) or a combination of groups (parents with teachers, teachers with governors, children with governors). A 'moan and groan' element is almost traditional at early meetings, and no bad thing at that – it usually reinforces the commonality of the challenge. It might also serve to lead into and focus upon what the community feels are the priority areas of concern and provide some tentative solutions. You might be brave enough to consider an 'introductory' whole school community meeting with the possibility of establishing working sub-groups. What is important is that all have an opportunity to contribute. A vital element to introduce at this early stage is 'expert' advice. This might be your local education psychologist, an advisory teacher, a member of the school staff or one from a neighbouring school who has attended a behaviour management course. A sense of ownership by those who are to implement and respond to a policy is vital.

The inclusion of the environmental element within the audit is not an optional extra. Behaviour does not occur in a vacuum. We have already stated that children have a right to a healthy, stimulating environment. Yet the vast majority of school buildings and playgrounds seem purpose built to encourage inappropriate behaviour. Cramped classrooms, restricted exists, winding staircases and dark and distant cloakrooms provide for both accident and opportunity. Three hundred children on flat, bleak, hard tarmac for a hectic fifteen minutes creates tensions and discontent. Nooks, crannies and 'behind the huts' are ideal venues for the nefarious; one hesitates to list the activities that might go on in such areas or to suggest any age relatedness. Asking the children might provide some startling data.

'Local Management' has provided a greater opportunity for schools to develop their own sites and buildings. Quite simple strategies such as carpeting corridors or soft furnishing communal areas has had dramatic effects on noise levels. The advice of experts – local authority architects and planners – is essential to avoid expensive mistakes. A parent with a lump hammer might be very willing to remove a partition wall and thereby extend the reception classroom, but beware, you might be a listed building – in more senses than one. Large-scale fixed playground apparatus is not the answer to all your breaktime problems. There is now a wealth of sound advice and practice in respect of school grounds and playground development and we have listed sources at the end of the chapter. Such a holistic approach to behaviour management is essential if it is to be effective. It also gives more scope for participation and provides for positive activity which, in itself, fosters good behaviour. Children who have been involved in designing and developing their own play spaces will make sure they are used appropriately.

Children Behave If They Know The Rules

The basis for the developing policy must be the rules under which all are to operate. Whether in school or the wider society, rules should clearly demonstrate that they are for the benefit of all – no rules for rules' sake, the only purpose of which is to subdue or control for control's sake.

Children need a simple, practical framework upon which to base their behaviour and a clear idea of what is and is not acceptable in a variety of settings. It is interesting to note that arguably those children from groups who have a strong religious and moral base find it much easier to accept the disciplines of school life than children whose early years lack any form of structure. Inner-city children who have become used to 'behaving' in the gurdwara, temple, church or mosque may fare better than children from the 'new' urban estates which often lack community spirit, have no established 'church' base and which, architecturally, negate any feeling of ownership. For some children, even the experiences and attendant etiquettes of family meals are absent. Children eat 'on the hoof' or whilst watching television. It is no small wonder they find it difficult to bridge the chasm between the normalities of home and school. To be told at home to 'hit back if someone hits you', and then to be punished at school for so doing may leave the child emotionally confused. Wider participation in the rule-making process can provide opportunities for open discussion on the philosophy behind the rules, and stress the importance of consistency.

That rules should be couched in positive terms and apply to all might be a new insight for parents and teachers. 'Listen carefully when anyone is talking to you' is for adult *and* child. Whilst 'don't punch or kick' might not be relevant for adults, those adults may not have thought of the more positive expression 'keep your hands and feet to yourself'.

For our purpose we need to make distinction between vague ideals and more specific rules. 'Being kind' or 'having a concern for others' are laudable aims to which we should all aspire, but they have limitations within a behaviour management context. Quite apart from being woolly concepts for children, they are not easily 'seen' and there is difficulty in assessing the degree of kindness or concern. On the other hand 'please walk when inside the school building' is an observable act which epitomises 'a concern for others'

One school has cleverly combined both ideals and rules in its behaviour document. Examples are:

● We must not harm each other; we will keep our hands and feet to ourselves.
● Our classroom is a place to care and share; we will push chairs under tables and replace books and equipment.

Within guide-lines, children are well able to negotiate their own rules, particularly in respect of their own classroom.

A feature which aids management and memory is to design rules that are few in number and 'comprehensive' in that they will apply at all times of day (Canter, 1992). For example, 'do as you are told first time' is not only observable but overarching in respect of time, place and activity. You do not need a multitude of written rules which extol children to 'sit quietly on the carpet for a story' or 'line up quietly in the playground'. Once the 'do as you are told first time' rule has been established, children are expected to follow whatever instruction is given. Such rules are also applicable across teachers and carers – whoever gives an instruction must be obeyed.

There will be a need for 'around the school' rules. 'Please walk within the school building' covers a multitude of sins – running, jumping, sliding, whirling – in a multitude of places. Those which are particularly pertinent to the lunch-break may be negotiated and established by working parties of, say, children supervisors and delegated teachers.

Displaying rules clearly in relevant areas not only reminds the children but also provides references for all staff, particularly anyone new to the school or working on a temporary basis. It is a great comfort to a supply teacher to be able to point to a large notice on the wall which states, 'We raise our hand to answer a question'. There is no protracted debate or confusion about the expectations of the permanent, but absent, class teacher.

In summary, a few clearly stated universal rules developed with common consent are more likely to succeed than those which are prescribed. However, their success depends upon the consistency and fairness of their application. Rules are there to be kept, but we all know that they are going to be broken. It is as important to know what will happen if the rules are kept as it is to know what will happen if they are not.

Children Behave Because Of What They Might Get

As the Elton Report states, '...the best way to encourage good standards of behaviour in a school is a clear code of conduct backed by a balanced combination of rewards and punishments within a positive community atmosphere.' (ibid 4:40 HMSO, 1989) So crucial is the term 'combination' that the issues of rewards and punishments are better considered together. That should not imply a carrot and stick approach. The reason for their interrelatedness has to do with a word that Elton failed to highlight – *choice*. Once the children have negotiated the rules with you, it must be made abundantly clear that it is their choice as to whether or not to follow those rules. If they choose to act appropriately, then they are rewarded – or 'positively reinforced' (Canter, ibid.). Should they choose not to 'obey', then they must accept the consequences. The onus is therefore on the child. Children are responsible for their own actions and *earn* the consequences. What is also important is that the consequences, for both good behaviour and inappropriate behaviour, must be clear to all from the outset and, once earned, cannot be revoked.

Many teachers are recognising the need for comprehensive and structured reward systems which range from verbal praise to a meal at a local fast-foods chain. Whatever the reward, it must have value for the child. That value can be anything from a verbal acknowledgement of appropriate behaviour, a star or sticker, certificates which accumulate to a book prize or 'good behaviour notes' to take home. (NPC, 1990:Canter, ibid.)

Mindful of teachers' pockets, we see no reason why schools should not purchase a 'stock' of small prizes to be given when children reach a certain number of team points. Sweets are not recommended, but bulk buying of such items as pens, pencils, rubbers, pencil sharpeners and small notebooks may be cost effective as well as educational. It is recognised that the value can be age specific. Nursery and reception teachers find it easier to provide 'valuable' rewards than their secondary colleagues. A four year old will find a smiley face sticker a lot more agreeable than a Year 6 student. However, for the older pupil there may be the possibility of 'free time', additional time on the computer, or even the opportunity to stay in the classroom during break instead of being shut out in the cold.

In the same way that rewards must have value to the child – they must be something the child likes – a 'negative consequence' (Canter, ibid.) must be something the child does not like. We are familiar with the children who enjoy being kept in at playtime, either because it's too cold outside or because it gives them a further opportunity to disrupt and gain attention.

Negative consequences, however, should not be vengeful. It is the negative behaviour we are hoping to eliminate, not the child. Nor should they be physically or psychologically harmful or demeaning, and where possible, be immediate. This might take the form of an immediate recording for a future consequence. For example, a missed playtime 'earned' near to 'home time' will have to be carried over to the next day.

Where possible, negative consequences should be restitutional, for example, cleaning off their own graffitti.

Above all, they should be ones the teacher is comfortable with using. (NPC, ibid; Canter, ibid.)

Negative consequences should be clearly stated and widely known. This is particularly important in respect of serious misbehaviour. No matter how well-ordered a school, there will be incidents of severe and/or persistent disruption or violence against persons and property which will necessitate the involvement of parents or carers. Objectivity is sustained if all parties are familiar with agreed pre-defined guidelines for action.

Schools should take care to grade sanctions relative to the level and/or frequency of inappropriate behaviour. Three missed playtimes might seem harsh for one-off jumping down the stairs, but inadequate for verbal abuse of a lunchtime supervisor. Further, it has been found that the effectiveness of sanctions lies not in their severity but in the consistency of application. A one minute 'keep back' when all the other children have gone out to play is effective if consistently and fairly applied by all members of staff.

We know, as adults, that we feel much better if we are praised than if we are criticised. Good managers know that recognising merit, even if it has to be dug for, builds morale. One head-teacher stated that he felt he had failed in his duty on days when he had not been into every classroom to praise the teacher and children for some piece of work or other creditable achievement. It also allows room, when and where necessary, for a ready acceptance of positive criticism.

Start the day by praising the children who enter the classroom quietly or are the first to settle down to work. You'll be surprised at how much better you feel, let alone the children.

If you make a conscious effort to praise and reward throughout the day, you will leave yourself much less room to be negative – but when you do have to admonish, it is noted! It is possible to praise every child every day. Scan the class just before 'home time' and make an effort to find something pleasant to say to anyone you may have missed out during the day.

Many schools use points system as a flexible and comprehensive means of immediately acknowledging a range of accomplishments. Points may be given for good work, effort, appropriate behaviour and punctuality. Points can be given at all times of the day, in all places and by all people. It is important that non-teaching assistants and lunchtime supervisors have the opportunity to reward. It not only makes their job easier but boosts their morale and status.

Points accumulate to set 'reward' targets. At the beginning of a new school year or term an easily reached target with a small prize or certificate encourages a good start. Targets can then be stretched as the term or year proceeds.

Whole class reward systems provide an opportunity to acknowledge whole class achievement. A class might receive a star or token for lining up well in the playground, walking down a corridor or keeping quiet in assembly. Stars and tokens can build to a target – ten stars gets you all (and your teacher) an extra playtime. Highlighting a class who have reached their target during assembly maintains interest and stimulates the others.

'Praise' and 'Congratulations' Assemblies are now commonplace in schools, but, apart from the retirement farewells, how many school think of regularly and publicly recognising the work of the crossing warden, the lunchtime supervisors or the school cooks? And what about a 'Cleaner's Award', presented by the cleaner for the tidiest classroom that month or a 'Secretary's Award' for the class that brings in all their dinner money on time?

Parents can also be praised, directly or indirectly. In some nurseries, if a child gets a 'well done' sticker, then mum, dad or carer gets one at collection time. Less obvious are good notes home which praise the child for a particular piece of work or good behaviour. Praise the child – praise the parent. Some schools have found this strategy so effective that two such notes must go home from every class every day (Canter ibid.). In a ten class school this means that twenty notes are going into the community each day. The news soon spreads that good things are happening in school and everyone feels good. It also makes the negative communications that must occasionally go home that much more effective and acceptable.

Conclusion: Everyone Behaves...if Everyone Knows

There must come a time when all your enquiry, all your thoughts, all your considerations must synthesise to a structure that is acceptable to the majority and clear and concise in its expression. Practicality is the name of the game and simplicity is the key. Many whole school behaviour policies are left on shelves to gather dust because they are too complicated, too full of do's and don'ts, too vague and idealistic.

A simple set of observable rules backed by an emphasis on positive reinforcement and reward for appropriate behaviour and a consistent, fair hierarchy of negative consequences of inappropriate behaviour within a caring and supportive structure must be the end point of your planning. Your next step is to find a means to introduce, explain and activate your policy.

For children, an introductory assembly – or assemblies – could feature salient points of *their* policy. Role play could help to emphasise what appropriate or inappropriate behaviour would earn. A special 'double points' week might start the policy with gusto.

For parents, a copy of the policy could disseminate information. A signed reply slip stating that the document had been read might prove useful for future reference. But what about a launch night for parents, carers and governors? This could lead to further parental/carer involvement. Schools have begun to recognise a need amongst parents for behaviour management training, and whole school behaviour documents have been a starting point for parent-teacher workshops which address those needs.

One word of warning. No matter how thoughtful and considered has been your planning, the policy in practice might need adjustment or refinement. Continued monitoring and reviews at regular intervals can ensure that the policy remains relevant, effective – and remembered!

....If Everyone Is Cared For

Policies should be a starting point for, and extend to encompass, the 'extra' needs of those particular children within school who find it difficult to cope. The Child Therapy Trust has stated that there are, on average, three children in every class in Britain in need of psychotherapeutic support (Child Psychotherapy Trust, 1990). Given that, nationally, the number of child psychotherapists is limited, there is an onus upon schools to do all that they can to help such children. Effective strategies have included:

1 'programmed' counselling sessions with children and counselling surgeries for both parent and child (the latter taking place after school hours and undertaken by an experienced member of staff);
2 the use of a 'nominated' teacher system, whereby children with particular problems are assigned a teacher. This is usually, but not always, the child's class teacher. Should any incident involving the child occur, the child is immediately taken to the nominated teacher, to ensure a consistent and balanced response;
3 anger management techniques, where working through local educational psychologists and/or advisory and social work services, children have been able to

articulate their feelings of anger. This might simply mean marking a cross on a body plan to show where they feel anger or modelling expressions in clay. This leads to an understanding of anger as a natural response and to an exploration of how anger may be expressed positively.

4 the development of anti-bullying strategies – for both bullying and bullied – which have encouraged the use of the 'one warning and report' rule. The child being bullied is encouraged to tell the bully – just once – to desist, otherwise a teacher will be told. If the bully does not desist, the bullied child must report the bullying. The key is an immediate response from the adult informed. A corollary to the rule is that, if no action has been taken by the informed adult, the child should seek out a second adult (NPC, 1993).

All children need to have self-esteem fostered and developed. It is particularly important for those who, through no fault of their own, are gripped by low self-esteem. Effective reward systems within your policy will do much in this respect, but more can be done for all children through specific programmes. The 'Circle Time' approach gives children the opportunity to express a wide range of attitudes, needs and feelings in a protected environment. For example, one feature of Circle Time is 'Special Person for the Day'. All children in the class are given the opportunity throughout the term to be the 'Special Person for the Day'. The other children will find good things to say about the special person and may suggest a suitable treat (Mosley, 1993, White 1992).

....If Everyone Is Committed

Building and developing a whole school behaviour policy costs time, effort and money. There is no doubting teacher effort and, if you are serious, time can be found. Money may be another matter. As suggested, the purchase of small prizes, a supply of certificates and stickers is not beyond the reach of the poorest school. Similarly the provision of teacher materials necessary to introduce such ideas as 'Circle Time' is not exorbitant, and even the support of 'extra' professionals to inaugurate anger management programmes may be cost-effective. However, if you are into a complete redevelopment of your school grounds and buildings to make it more child comfortable, you must be aware of the long-term financial implications, not only for the initial funding, but for the necessary maintenance.

Many schools now supply inexpensive small apparatus which is 'counted out' and 'counted in' each lunchtime.

One school makes use of a classroom adjacent to the playground for indoor lunchtime activities – painting, crayoning, pasting. Lunchtime supervisors oversee the room on a rota basis. Supervisors take a real pride in the work achieved and are allowed to display it on the walls. They are even bringing in their own 'scrap' materials.

'Table' games in each classroom – kept in sturdy plastic boxes – provide activity for the children and respite for the supervisor at wet lunchtimes!

Most importantly, schools have invited lunchtime supervisors to 'teacher days' when behaviour management is on the agenda. Supervisors have the opportunity to gain insights into more general behaviour management techniques and also to contribute fully to workshops specific to the lunchtime break (NPC, 1993).

....If Everyone Has Been Valued

There is perhaps no other area of school life where children, parents, teachers and the wider community share common ground in respect of their own needs than that of relationships. Children *do* want to behave and they want others to behave well towards them. Parents and teachers want their children to behave, and want to know how to make them behave. Governors want to be seen to be governing a good school. Local people want to take a pride in the institutions within their neighbourhood. Working together, based upon a common need and driven by a common purpose, builds positive relationships. It will be those very relationships, founded on a respect for and a value of others, that are the essence of a good behavioural policy – and good health!

This chapter is dedicated to the memory of Hazel Wright, Head Teacher of Grove Infant School, Birmingham.

CHAPTER 8

Developing and Implementing Policy and Curriculum Through Action Research

Kay Danai

Introduction

For several years as Co-ordinator of Health Education in a first school, I felt that I was not carrying out my role in a satisfactory and fulfilling way. I wanted to find a means of developing a programme of health education that would be relevant and meaningful to all those concerned and which would raise the profile of the school as a 'health-promoting school'. My intention was not simply to produce a written policy or document stating priorities for the future, although this was a direct result of my research, but also to increase general awareness of health issues within the context of education.

I believe that, during the time that we are involved in teaching and learning, each and every one of us generates our own theories about professional practice. These are invariably influenced by writers, researchers and educationalists but, more importantly, by our own practice. Often, subconsciously, we reflect upon our teaching and make personal and private resolutions to 'do it better next time' or 'try another approach' or even 'forget it altogether'! We plan, we reflect, we modify and then we take the most appropriate course of action. In so doing we are being 'self-reflective' practitioners. We are recognising that something which we believed to be effective, successful or beneficial may, in fact, need to be refined and adapted in various ways. Rather than have doubts and push them aside, we make a conscious effort to do something in order to bring about an improvement.

If we are prepared to go one step further and share some of our own discoveries with others, we offer colleagues the possibility of seeking new ways to approach their own teaching. By making this public we are, in effect, involved in a process of 'researching' our practice, of investigating ways and means of improving it and thereby contributing in a valuable way to theories of education.

Practitioner-based research or, more specifically, 'action research', demands the same rules of rigour and validity as any other type of research. The enquiry must be systematic and made public (Stenhouse, 1975) so that it is open to analysis and critique. Frequently the area chosen to be studied is one in which we feel that our own professional theories are not in line with our practice. In other words we say one thing but do another. Whitehead (1984) refers to this as 'living contradiction' which needs to be addressed by confronting it and finding ways to make improvements.

Why I Chose Action Research

For me action research was the most appropriate process of enquiry to adopt if I wanted to bring about long-term improvements in the teaching of health education within my school. There were certain qualities inherent in this approach that appealed to me.

A focus on personal practice

Action research is grounded in personal practice. It is concerned with improving oneself and extending oneself both personally and professionally. The fundamental aim of action research is to improve the quality of practice (Elliott, 1991). The process of education, the 'whys and hows' of what we do become a central focus.

In the process of devising a programme of health education for my school, I was aiming to focus on the *ways* and *means* of approaching health education within the classroom and, as a *result* of my research, to produce a bank of ideas, materials and resources that would form the knowledge base of a health education curriculum.

A focus on values

Action research is explicitly value laden. Lomax (1990) states:

> Action research incorporates the examination and refinement of the educational values that we hold in an attempt to make them central to practice. A starting point for action research is to clarify our values in the area in which we wish to bring about improvement.

I believe that consciously raising our awareness by openly and honestly discussing these values, brings us one step closer towards developing a shared understanding of how and why we teach as we do. Understanding what *really* matters to the children in our care and using this to initiate discussion and develop a sense of sharing and tolerance becomes of paramount importance.

A focus on subjectivity

In the same way that objective, quantitative research methods are well suited to particular situations and research questions, I feel that a qualitative, more subjective approach, which I chose to adopt in my study, suited the research that I was undertaking. This was because my primary aim was not simply to collect data with a view to interpreting and analysing it (although that did form part of my research methodology) but, more significantly, to *bring about changes* in my teaching as my enquiry progressed. It necessarily had to be subjective and I wanted it that way. Having said that, I was aware of a need for an element of objectivity and so I invited others to judge the rigour and validity of my research.

A focus on collaboration and ownership

Implicit in action research is the notion of collaboration and shared ownership of the research. Rudduck (1991) writes,

> Some sense of ownership of the agenda for action is a good basis for professional development and professional learning.

It requires individuals to make findings known and to encourage others to participate in the development of the research by voicing their thoughts and expressing their concerns. Necessarily the teacher researcher has to expose educational values and practices and be open to scrutiny. The process of initiating a health education programme was, for me, only the beginning of a longer term plan which, to be successful, required the commitment and support of colleagues.

My Action Plan

Having chosen to pursue an action research approach to my study, I then decided to draw up an 'action plan' to lead me into the first cycle of the process. This was based on the following six critical questions posed by Whitehead and Foster in 1984:

1 What was my concern?
2 Why was I concerned?
3 What did I think I could do about it?
4 What kind of evidence could I collect to help me make some kind of judgement about what was happening?
5 How could I collect such evidence?
6 How would I check that my judgement about what had happened was reasonably fair and accurate?

This gave me some kind of structure and a point of referral when necessary. It also helped me to think about each stage of development and to plan the next step accordingly. It did *not* mean that each cycle in the research process was clear cut or prescriptive. I understood that allowances had to be made for hiccups and surprises but at least it gave me a sense of direction and kept the work focused.

I would like to share this with you as an example of a possible way to approach an action research enquiry within school.

What was my concern?

Health education was not co-ordinated well within the school. There was no policy or practical guidelines. Teachers depended upon their own, often limited, knowledge and rarely sought guidance from myself. This suggested to me that either colleagues were unsure as to what was expected of them, or even rather complacent in their attitudes towards teaching of health education. I strongly believed that the existing situation could be improved.

Why was I concerned?

Health education was rarely given the attention it deserved within the school. Many aspects of health education were not being addressed simply because staff were unaware of them. Lack of time, experience and resources were cited as reasons for neglecting the teaching of important issues such as drug abuse and sex education. Although guidance had been offered by the former National Curriculum Council (1991) and various authorities had produced guide-lines aimed at improving general awareness, my belief was that the message was not being received. There was still a degree of confusion regarding the exact nature of health education and how best to approach a host of topics and issues.

What did I think I could do about it?

My principle aim was to motivate members of staff to recognise the value of health education to children's learning and to incorporate it more frequently into their practice. I wanted to emphasise cross-curricular links and to assure colleagues that, with careful planning, this 'additional' subject may not be regarded as such. Rather I wanted it to be seen as an extension and elaboration of current good practice.

What kind of evidence could I collect to help me make some kind of judgement about what was happening?

There were four crucial steps:

  a) Assessment of my own classroom practice and the extent to which I incorporated health education in my teaching. I knew that I did not practise what I preached! I was not living out my educational values and I wanted to change this situation.
  b) A request for help from colleagues in assessing their own attitudes, values, and beliefs. It was very important for me to determine how members of staff approached the teaching of health education and how individual priorities and internal politics affected this.
  c) An analysis of the quantity and quality of resources within the school and the familiarity of colleagues with these resources. This would involve the

compilation of a resource guide/list.

d) An assessment of how parents and governors regarded health education. This would involve requesting views on health education and suggestions for a health education programme.

How could I collect such evidence?

a) Careful monitoring of my own teaching to include field notes on the amount of time spent on health education and a record of the nature of that teaching.

b) Staff curriculum meetings. These would be formal and informal. They would be tape recorded with the consent of all those present and reflected upon by myself at a later date. Questionnaires would also be used to gather opinions and suggestions.

c) Liaison with health education/promotion departments. This would help me to assess the resources currently available and the suitability of those resources for our school. It would also involve discussions with members of these departments on aspects of curriculum planning.

d) Requests for parents and governors to air their views. This would include questionnaires and informal discussions.

How would I check that my judgement about what had happened was reasonably fair and accurate?

From the outset I decided to identify several 'critical friends', people who would openly and honestly give me feedback on my enquiry as the programme was initiated. This included a colleague at school, a headteacher from a primary school, and a friend involved in health promotion. It also involved liaison with both the County Adviser for Personal, Social and Health Education and the District Health Promotion Manager. As my work was also being assessed as part of a college degree course I had the benefit of lecturers' comments as well. My aim was to validate my enquiry as it progressed and ensure that it was as rigorous and valid as possible.

As I moved from analysing my own classroom practice to involving other members of staff, including non-teaching staff, in the policy making process, I would use their comments and criticisms to help structure future plans. This would help me validate my findings as I progressed and, I hoped, reduce the risk of any misperceptions.

I also intended to use the children as a source of validation. Since my classroom practices would be restructured to a certain extent, the children would be encouraged to make comments regarding the changes. I was certain that, at nine years of age, they would be capable of making constructive suggestions and of reflecting upon the work covered. This would include the tape recording of discussions and the use of diaries. My own notes would supplement this.

A detailed account of how I put my entire action plan into operation is documented fully in my dissertation (Danai, 1993). However, I have selected three of the most significant areas to illustrate my research in practice.

The Role of Children

I decided to devote the first six weeks of my study to the children in my class, to reflect upon and assess the quality of my work as it progressed and then to make a decision as to the next stage of development according to how I perceived the situation.

I chose to adopt a cross-curricular approach to the health education work that I intended to cover because I considered this to be the most effective way of approaching the range of issues ahead of me. In particular I wanted to focus on the role that the core subject of English could play in developing health education. The involvement of the children in my research was of paramount importance to me and the notion of encouraging children to participate in a partnership role and to be more responsible for their own learning became an intrinsic part of the process. How, then, did I begin?

The development of a theme

I chose 'Keeping Myself Safe' as the theme for the first six weeks of my study. This linked well with weekly visits by the police who were running a safety programme for local schools.

I wanted to discover, right from the outset, the children's perceptions of this area of study and so I decided to adopt the 'Draw and Write Investigation' technique (Williams, Wetton, and Moon, 1989). This was introduced to me on a health education in-service course two years earlier as an effective way of discovering what children know and believe about health. It involved the use of carefully structured questions to find out how much the children already knew about particular issues.

The children were encouraged to draw pictures and to write sentences based on their knowledge and experience.

For the purpose of my theme, I asked the children to draw a picture of a 'safe' place. No clues were given, no discussion took place. Once they had completed the task, I asked them to draw a picture of the thing(s) from which they were keeping safe. Again no help was given. They were encouraged to write one or two sentences about the pictures if they wished. At the end of the activity I invited them to share their work with the other children and to discuss it.

Most of their pictures were of a fantasy nature – monsters, dragons, aliens, ghosts, etc, whilst others were based on real dangers such as strangers, burglars and fire. We compiled a list of 'real' dangers and 'imaginary' dangers and as part of an art lesson, the children created a large frieze of their fears together with red warning triangles depicting real dangers. We discussed the procedures in cases of emergency and I developed this theme further by using 'What...if?' cards in drama. These were a set of hypothetical situations requiring the children to act out, in groups, the scenes and their solutions to them. For example, one card asked the children to imagine that they were walking along the street when, suddenly, they saw smoke coming from a bedroom window. What would they do? Another asked them how they would react to an accident in the home or to finding a young child who was lost.

We also developed the theme of imaginary fears by creating an expressive dance to music which culminated in the children pushing aside and overcoming their worst fears. This was later performed in front of the school as part of a class assembly on 'Keeping Ourselves Safe'.

Back in the classroom, I decided to introduce fiction to our study in the form of two popular children's stories. *Not now, Bernard* by D.McKee and *I'm Coming to Get You!* by T. Ross. Both are humorous stories which the children began to discuss as soon as I had read them. I wanted to use the stories as a stimulus for discussing the children's responses to unsafe or threatening situations but, at the same time, not to cause unnecessary anxiety.

The children suggested ways and means of coping with the dilemmas faced by the characters in the stories. Following my desire to develop the language aspect of health education, I then asked the children to write their own stories based on *Not Now, Bernard* in groups of four or five. During the weeks that followed they revised and re-drafted their scripts until they were satisfied and then produced a book in the same format as the original. Each child, according to their level of ability within the group took responsibility for certain pages and the rest of the group checked for spelling mistakes, punctuation, etc. Using a peer approach to the work was a deliberate attempt to encourage collaboration and to increase the children's self-esteem. The completed books were taken to another class, with a set of questions devised by the children, and read to 'reading partners' for their reactions. This gave a purpose for writing and an audience with whom they could share their work.

As part of my research I asked the children to keep diaries and to comment upon the work being covered. I also tape recorded sessions so that I could reflect upon them at a later date. I wanted to capture the flavour of the children's thoughts and this brought with it a realisation that issues which I had not intended to raise often emerged during discussions. By adopting a teaching strategy that begins with what the child already knows and which develops from a very personal knowledge, I discovered that there was a depth of understanding and a potential to explore issues that I had not anticipated.

For some teachers, perhaps, the very uncertainty of this approach may be threatening. It requires, I discovered, a willingness to meet the children at their own level, to show that you are seeking to understand them and not to be judgemental. Above all it allows you to develop a genuine concern for the children's thoughts and feelings and to understand them better as a result.

During one school year, the time in which I was developing the health education programme, I continued to incorporate health related themes into my planning. We covered an array of subjects including feelings, friendships, medicines and drugs, growing up and others. Themes became inter-related and evolved from one another. The children compiled a list of topics which they considered to be particularly important to learn about and I incorporated these into the programme when it was devised. I also compared the children's suggestions with those made by colleagues and parents and found that, whilst there were some differences, there were also some striking similarities which I shall highlight later.

The Role of Colleagues

Throughout my research I was aware that my own professional development would ultimately affect the development of the school as a whole. In developing my own theories in practice, with the intention of sharing these with others, I was anticipating a shift in thinking on the part of the staff and a change in policy on the part of those in positions of management. With regard to this, I believe that the culture in which a researcher is working becomes critical to the success or failure of such research enterprise. Hargreaves and Hopkins (1991) write,

> Successful schools realise that development planning is about creating a school culture which will support the planning and management of changes of many different kinds.

As my enquiry progressed I realised that I was in a very favourable environment for the development of a health education programme through action research. The staff were supportive and open to suggestions as to how they might improve their teaching of health related topics. There was, however, scepticism amongst some colleagues regarding the amount of time that this would take, bearing in mind the heavy demands of the National Curriculum. My aim, therefore, was to offer ways of incorporating health education into on-going work. I did not want this to be perceived as an additional 'burden'. With careful planning, I believed that we could implement a well co-ordinated health education programme which would not detract from valuable work already taking place, but rather enrich it.

I needed to develop a shared understanding of aims and objectives with colleagues. I wanted them to look closely at their practice and to question what they were teaching and why. I used several curriculum meetings to identify areas of concern, to look at resources, to discuss links with other curriculum subjects and to share my own experiences within the classroom. Members of staff spoke openly about their priorities and the areas of health education which they considered to be most important. Throughout these sessions I emphasised the cross-curricular nature of health education and, in particular, the potential of using language-based activities, not only to fulfil the requirements of the National Curriculum Orders, but also to bring more personal meaning to the children's work.

Gradually, over a period of several months, we arrived at a common understanding of needs and wants. There was, however, still a question of balance and co-ordination. In order for the final programme to be effective, topics would either have to be linked to existing schemes of work, integrated into Core subject areas or treated as a subject in their own right. There was also a need for progression across all age groups. I therefore organised a teacher education day to focus upon whole school planning and, with the help of colleagues, identified those areas of health education which would form part of the programme. Each year group linked topics to existing schemes of work wherever possible and it was my responsibility to incorporate other topics into an overall framework.

We also discussed the ways in which our school could become health-promoting. It was agreed, for example, to take a closer look at what we encouraged the children to eat during break times. Similarly, we discussed the general environment and issues such as cleanliness, the ethos of the school, the role of non-teaching members of staff, the 'hidden curriculum' and the development of positive relationships within the school and with parents and members of the community. We decided to carry out an audit of the school ethos and environment using the 'Health-Promoting School' diagram (Lloyd & Morton, 1992) as a guide. This enabled us to assess the stage which we had reached and where we were aiming to be in twelve months' time. It gave a focus and a structure to our plans and it supplemented advice given to staff by the County Adviser for Personal, Social and Health Education who had been invited to the school to make her own assessment two months previously. As a result of our discussions we were able to draw up a list of priorities and to set an agenda for the following months.

All in all the day was very productive, much being covered, not only in terms of the curriculum, but also whole school issues.

The Role of Parents

Perhaps one of the most rewarding parts of the research, for me, focused on the parents. I decided early on in my study that I would request their help whenever possible, recognising that a working partnership between parents and teachers can help to ensure that children are given clear, consistent messages (TACADE 1990). I therefore arranged to attend a Parents' Association meeting to put forward my proposals and to give those present a questionnaire. This was an invitation to parents to air their views regarding the teaching of health education and to gain an insight into what they believed health education to involve. As a result of their responses I then sent further questionnaires to a larger number of parents (one third of the school's population).

The replies were very revealing! All too often, it seems, we assume that we know what parents think and feel. We congratulate ourselves on forming links with parents by inviting them into school to help with reading, cooking, maths activities and so forth. Rarely, however, do we ask them how they *feel* about the things we teach. There is, I believe, a role for parents in voicing their thoughts in a constructive way and assuring them that their opinions will be taken into consideration.

I received a wealth of information from the parents, many of them giving me much more than I had requested. Their response provided me with the opportunity to look for similarities and differences, not only in their views, but, more significantly, in my views and those of my colleagues. I was made aware of issues that I had not recognised and sensed a depth of feeling towards this area of the curriculum that I had not anticipated.

As well as asking parents to outline their perceptions of health education, I also asked them to use an enclosed list of possible health education topics (such as dental health, safety, bullying, food, sex education, loss and death, etc) to indicate those issues which they considered to be important for children to learn about. They were also asked to indicate which of the topics they felt were unsuitable for first school children.

Dear Parents,

During the next academic year I shall be engaged in some research on health education and its role within our school. I would like to include a parental perspective and would very much appreciate your help with the following.

1) What do you understand by the term 'health education'?
2) Do you feel that health education, as you perceive it, should be included in the curriculum?
3) Inside the attached envelope is a list of topics which may be included in a health education programme. Please open it and indicate which of the topics you consider to be very important for children at this school to learn about.
4) Are there any topics which you would consider to be unsuitable for the children in this school?
Please list them.
5) If Yes, have you any particular reason for this?

Thank you for your help. If you would like to make any other comments, please feel free to scribble your thoughts in the space below.

So How Did The Parents Respond?

Of those surveyed, 69 per cent responded. With the exception of one respondent, all believed that health education should be an integral part of the children's curriculum. The parent who expressed a negative response in the words, 'When I was at primary school we didn't study "trendy" subjects but concentrated on the 3 R's...', interestingly, reviewed his/her perception of health education as the questionnaire progressed! Generally speaking, responses were positive and included such comments as, 'Having seen the list of topics I now realise that health education covers a great deal more than I first thought and I believe even more strongly that it should be included at first school.'

There were, however, reservations expressed by some parents regarding certain topics. Sixty-nine per cent listed some topics as unsuitable for first school children. The 'top five' for example were:

1 Aids
2 Sex/Sexuality
3 Menstruation
4 Puberty
5 Loss and death.

Reasons given for this were varied but tended to focus on protecting the 'innocence' of children for as long as possible.

Areas of health education that parents considered to be very important for children to learn about were as follows:

1 Road safety
2 Dental health
3 Keeping myself safe
4 Bullying
5 How my body works
6 Water safety
7 Exercise
8 Food
9 Helping others
10 Conservation

Having the children's response to a similar questionnaire enabled me to see some fascinating correlations. For example, 'road safety' also appeared at the top of the children's list. The topics of 'bullying' and 'keeping myself safe' were considered to be important, as were 'friendship' and 'health'. However, unlike many of the parents, the topics of 'sex education' and 'drugs' appeared on the children's list and they were able to explain to me why they felt that these were important subjects. Many of them seemed very aware of issues involved in both subjects and brought into question the presumed 'innocence' of many of the children by parents. This has also been the finding of other research looking at children's knowledge and understanding of health related issues (Williams, Wetton and Moon, 1989), and highlights the need to treat children as key participants in any debate regarding the promotion of health within school.

As previously stated, both views of parents and children were taken into consideration and incorporated into the programme. Both proved to be a very valuable source of information and helped to create a shared understanding of what we were hoping to achieve.

Conclusion

If I were to liken my experience of action research to any other experience in my life, it would probably be that of my first visit to a Cantonese restaurant! For this reason, the fully detailed version of my research is divided into six sections, each one dealing with a different aspect of the enquiry. Suffice to say that both experiences were a move away from the familiar, both were very enjoyable and both brought with them a number of surprises!

To 'would be' action researchers, or even colleagues interested in adopting a similar approach to myself, may I offer the following three pieces of advice?
Be open and honest about your personal approach to health issues within the classroom and curriculum.

Be prepared for a degree of resistance from members of staff who believe that health promotion is best left to health 'professionals'.

Be willing to stake your claim to a slice of the school budget and to convince others, through your own enthusiasm, of the value of health education.

I reflect upon the work that I carried out within my school with satisfaction and a sense of fulfilment. For me the experience of initiating and implementing a health education programme through action research was both personally rewarding and professionally worthwhile. The process was both a shared and meaningful one. As the programme works through its first year, I believe that the foundations have been laid for the children to enjoy a fuller, more enriched curriculum and, I hope, to experience health education at its best within a health-promoting school.

CHAPTER 9

The National Curriculum and the Health-Promoting Primary School

John Lloyd

Introduction

The health education curriculum has an important place in the promotion of health in schools and is firmly established as a Cross-Curricular Theme (NCC 1990a) (NCC 1990b) and a component of Science in the National Curriculum (DES 1991) for England and Wales. Similar curriculum guidance for health education has also been established for Northern Ireland (NICC 1990) and Scotland (SHEG 1990).

It is ironic that the Ministry of Education (HMSO 1956) first drew attention to the importance of health education as part of the formal and incidental curricula of schools thirty years ago and not necessarily as a subject but covering, 'a definite and demanding field of subject matter'.

It is even more ironic that just as Dearing (1993) is presently attempting to reduce 'curriculum overload' the Ministry then commented that,

> too many timetables are too full as it is; in any case health education if it is going on all the time, may not invariably lend itself to condensation into one or two short weekly periods.

The pressure on the timetable and the competition for curriculum time is as great today as it was then! However, as HMI (1986), and later, the National Curriculum Council argued (1990b), the Ministry clearly recognised that health education required as much thought and careful planning as any other subject.

> For teachers who realise the possibilities and importance of the subject, invaluable opportunities will suggest themselves in the course of teaching other subjects.

Lewis (1993) asserts that subjects such as biology, PE and history have always provided opportunities to deliver health education in a cross-curricular way, but suggests that total reliance on such an approach may call into question the integrity of specific subjects and may well be 'haphazard, fragmented and lacking in any coherent planned progression'. He rightly points out that to avoid such reliance many schools mix cross-curricular approaches to health education with discrete lessons on specific health related topics and themes.

The Department for Education and Science (DES 1977) in the wake of the Court Report (1977) on children's health emphasised that health education is central to the role of schools and their aims, especially in,

> the skills and academic areas across the curriculum...it is a central part of the role of every teacher and cannot be left to certain departments in schools or certain teachers.

It is important to note that successive guidance (HMI 1986, NCC 1990b, HEA 1993) has highlighted the health education curriculum not only for its academic contribution to pupils' knowledge and understanding, but also for the skills necessary for developing self-esteem, well-being and ultimately health. Such guidance does much to emphasise that health education is an essential part of every pupil's entitlement and that the development of skills will help individuals to use their knowledge about health effectively. Moreover, the European Resolution on Education and Health (EC 1989), and the subsequent European Network of Health-Promoting Schools Project, recognise the important contribution that subjects of the curriculum can make to the acquisition of health-promoting attitudes and knowledge. In order for a school to be health-promoting it should provide 'a stimulating and well balanced health education curriculum'. (HEA 1993)

The centrality of the development of self-esteem and well-being to the content and the process of health education is self-evident for as Tones (1987) asserts, the goal of self-empowerment in developing genuine informed choices is an essential life skill and component of personal and social education. 'Personal and social education in the school context is inextricably linked with health education'.

In the promotion of health in the primary school, the symbiotic relationship between life-skills teaching and social education in Tones's assertion, is as important as the symbiotic relationship between health education and health promotion.

In all of this, however, teachers must not lose sight of the fact that they bring their own attitudes and values to their teaching of health education. Neutral stances are impossible and it is difficult for any teacher engaged in health education to avoid subscribing to or even openly supporting particular values (Hyland 1988). Fear of indoctrination or indeed of the inculcation in pupils of the values of 'a healthy mind in a healthy body' (NCC 1990a) – to believe uncritically – is of concern. It draws attention to the need for teachers to be aware of their own values; to recognise the different ways in which particular types of health education may impact upon their teaching and pupils' learning, and upon their understanding of health as it is taught through the subjects of the curriculum.

It's Not What You Do, It's The Way That You Do It!

For many practitioners in primary schools best practice in health education is as much, or indeed more, about teaching and learning as it is about content. That is to say, it is about engaging pupils in participative activities which will enable them to explore their own feelings and attitudes towards health matters, to practise skills and increasingly to reflect upon their own health-related behaviours. Ultimately such an approach is seen as a legitimate way of enabling pupils to make choices about present and future lifestyles.

However, there are those who consider that school should simply be engaged in telling pupils how to behave, what they should or should not do, prescribing or coercing particular forms of health behaviour on the grounds that adults know best. Such paternal authoritarianism, although well intentioned, is misplaced and of concern since it has little to do with education.

Jones (1988) reviews this dichotomy in her consideration of health education approaches which can be broken down under three headings as: coercive preventative; educational preventative; radical preventative.

The coercive preventative or health risk approach is very much about informing and advising pupils to change or modify their behaviour. It is strongly supported by medical facts and opinion and often taught through 'shock/horror' tactics (i.e. pictures of diseased lungs and dead heroin addicts).

Such an approach seeks to persuade pupils not to indulge in unhealthy activities. It seeks to prevent those things deemed as unhealthy through restriction of choice, legislation and discipline. In a primary school such a programme will be didactic in style – teacher taught making use of a video, or by visitors preaching a particular health message. Leaflets and posters will be much in evidence with little involvement if any by the learner in the process. Such an approach, as Lloyd (1991) notes,

> serves only to highlight a negative view of health and for many will reinforce their perception that health education is about adults telling them how to behave in order to stop them having fun.

The educational preventative or educational rational approach provides pupils with access to information about health issues in order to promote greater understanding. It engages the pupils in discussion, explores values and attitudes, and develops decision-making skills. Such an approach may well make use of direct teaching, audio-visual aids, visits and contributions from visitors, but in the primary classroom it will involve pupils in games, simulations, case studies, role plays, problem-solving exercises, surveys, open-ended questions and sentences, and group work of various kinds (NCC 1990b).

If pupils are increasingly to take some control over their own lives as they grow and mature into adulthood, then the importance of this development of 'life-skills' is very significant (Tones 1987, Tones 1993, Anderson 1988). The notion of self-empowerment through the development of self-esteem, positive self-image, clear values and goals, and assertiveness is central to this. The process is not confined to health education alone in the primary school, it can be developed throughout the curriculum and is a major contributor to the school ethos. Jones (1988) remarks that such an approach, 'raises the importance of self-esteem and self actualisation and effective programmes to promote informed decision-making and autonomy'.

To be effective, she continues, 'they require the promotion of true participatory and collaborative group discussion which incorporates consideration towards others'.

Jones recognises that unless teachers are trained in such approaches, utilising the same processes they are expected to use in their classroom, then they are likely to be unsuccessful. Donahue (1991a, 1991b) also notes that teachers of health education may need further training in the use of teaching methods based on the active involvement of pupils if they are to be effective in the classroom.

Lastly, the radical preventative or action for change approach to health education is very practical in the sense that it seeks to change organisations and communities in order to facilitate healthier choices. It also seeks to address inequalities in health through development of self-empowerment, encouraging and enabling individuals, groups and indeed whole communities to challenge those institutions, practices and vested interests which militate against health.

In a health-promoting primary school this approach would on the one hand ensure that the canteen provided not only healthy food choices but also a physical environment and atmosphere conducive to healthy eating. On the other, it would enable parents to participate more fully in the life of the school, by becoming the focus for campaigns on health issues as they affect the school and its community. For example, campaigning for traffic-calming measures outside school or pollution controls on local factories.

Inevitably, primary schools use elements of each approach but if pupils are to develop the appropriate skills necessary to participate fully, to make reasoned choices and be assertive then they will need plenty of opportunities in school to do so. Information alone will be insufficient, coercion is inappropriate, and restricting choice without a valid educational reason, no matter how well intentioned, is more about doing something for or to people rather than enabling them to take more control over their own lives (Lloyd 1991).

Curriculum Guidance 5: Health Education (NCC 1990b) for England and Wales recognises that the provision and acquisition of knowledge alone is unlikely to promote healthy behaviour and change unhealthy behaviour.

> If a health education programme is to help make informed choices, establish a healthy lifestyle and build up a system of values, the teaching methods used are as important as the content of the lessons. The participation of the pupils is essential in order to encourage pupils to learn from others and to help them use appropriate language in ways that are understood by others.

The guidance further recommends a balanced range of teaching methods and opportunities for pupils to:

assess evidence, make decisions, negotiate, listen, make and deal with relationships, solve problems and work independently and with confidence. While there is a place for direct teaching...much of teaching health education will be based on the active involvement of pupils.

This is compatible with advice previously given for personal and social education by Her Majesty's Inspectorate (1989) which commended these teaching and learning approaches in the classroom. As a principle, these are common to all the cross-curricular themes: Economic and Industrial Understanding, Health Education, Careers and Guidance, Environmental Education, and Citizenship. They promote attitudes, values and skills as part of pupils' entitlement to personal and social development as much as they deliver the content of each theme.

In The Classroom

Opportunities for teaching health education occur throughout the curriculum and are well illustrated in the relevant curriculum guidance documents for England and Wales, Scotland and Northern Ireland. Such is the importance of health education that it is specifically identified in the Attainment Targets and programmes of study for Science in the National Curriculum (DES 1991).

Attainment Target 2; Life and Living Process requires that at Key Stage 1 pupils should:

find out about themselves and develop their ideas about how they grow, feed, move, use their senses and about human development... and...should be introduced to ideas about how they keep healthy through exercise, personal hygiene, diet, rest and personal safety; and to the role of drugs as medicines. They should consider similarities between themselves and other pupils and understand that individuals are unique.

At Key Stage 2, pupils should:

explore ideas about processes of breathing, circulation, growth and reproduction...They should study how microbes and lifestyle can affect health including the defence systems of the body, diet, personal hygiene, safe handling of food, dental care and exercise. They should understand too the fact that while all medicines are drugs, not all drugs are medicines. They should begin to be aware of the harmful effect on health resulting from an abuse of tobacco, alcohol and other drugs.

Opportunities exist in the study of history to develop an understanding of health issues today. Changes in diet and nutrition during the 1930s and the Second World War are particularly relevant as is the study of the changing role of women in society during that period. Advances in medicine from the Ancient Greeks through to the development of penicillin and other life-saving drugs can be considered in the context of society's changing attitudes towards substance use, ranging from the extensive use of opium in the nineteenth century to the use of tobacco today. Changes in public health and medicine can be charted, whilst attitudes towards illness, disability and death can be explored through all periods. The important contribution of technology to health care through the ages covered by topics in history can also provide valuable insights for pupils.

The study of people and places can contribute to pupils' understanding of families, culture and society, of changes in health brought about by changes in population distribution and its effect on health service provision. The use of the coca plant as a cash crop in developing countries of South America is worthy of consideration, as pupils struggle to understand the complexities of the world of drugs.

The effects of pollution from industry, the inappropriate use of the environment, and the use of pesticides and nitrates on agricultural land may also develop pupils' attitudes towards their own health and concern for the health of others.

Religious education will always make an important contribution to health in primary school, providing a context for pupils to explore different faiths and beliefs within families and cultures. There will be opportunities to develop care, concern and respect for others, and as they grow, for pupils to consider the 'rites of passage', from childhood to adulthood. Birth, marriage and death can be sensitively approached through story, self-reflection and discussion.

The use of story in English can be used extensively to explore pupils' attitudes to and feelings about issues such as drugs, growing up, safety (including child protection and bullying) and health concerns of their own. Through speaking and listening to others the skills associated with decision making, problem solving and making and sustaining relationships can be developed and can be extended by the use of prose, poetry and drama.

Art, drama and music may all be used to explore feelings about contemporary health issues, behaviour and events as they affect pupils in their primary school and in their communities. Expressive arts can enable even the most reticent pupil to express emotion in a positive and supportive classroom.

Physical education by its very nature contributes to the health related exercise that all pupils in the primary school need. Opportunities to develop self-awareness, self confidence and self-esteem through individual, group and team activities, using floor space, apparatus, balls and parachutes games with pupils, are many and varied.

Although all subjects of the curriculum may make use of number, mathematics has a unique contribution to make. Pupils of all ages can collect and provide health related data about themselves and health matters as they affect them. Differences in height and weight as they grow, the foods they eat, unsafe places in their community, how fast they can run, their pulse rates, pollution around their environment and the leisure facilities they use can all provide insights into their health and lifestyle. It can provide problems to be solved and the evidence for changes necessary in order to lead healthier lives.

There are numerous curriculum resources and materials available to support health education in the primary school classroom. These provide appropriate teaching and learning strategies in order to develop not only knowledge, understanding and skills, but also to raise pupils self-concept, self-confidence and self-esteem.

The *Health For Life* resource (Williams, Wetton and Moon 1989a) explores the school as a health-promoting community and offers a progression for health education around growing and changing, keeping safe, medicines, healthy lifestyles, relationships, taking responsibility, feelings, bullying, growing up and substance abuse. Developed from their innovative research into children's beliefs about health (Williams Wetton and Moon 1990b), the resource identifies three key areas for health education: The World of Drugs, Keeping Myself Safe, Me and My Relationships. These provide ample opportunities for teachers to work in practical ways with their pupils and to explore feelings and attitudes, develop and practise skills and form healthy concepts.

Skills for the Primary School Child (TACADE 1990) and the *Supplementary Lesson Cards* (TACADE 1993) take a very skills-based approach to health education, emphasising the need for child protection in its broadest sense if children are to be safe, from drugs and bullies for example. The materials seek to raise self confidence and self-esteem through the development of personal and social skills in the classroom. The materials are supported by a manual which provides papers by experts on key issues and workshops for teachers and parents which support a whole school and community approach to health education. Recent research into the effectiveness of this approach suggests that the SPSC resource has been used very effectively throughout the country (Lloyd 1994). The Supplementary Cards offer specific lessons on health education and the other cross curricular themes which are especially suitable for pupils at Key Stage 2.

My Body Project (1991) offers a very structured, 'scientific' approach to health education for pupils between the ages of 9 and 12 years. Closely related to the Attainment Targets for Science, Mathematics and English, the materials explore the themes of air, what you are made of, the need for oxygen, body systems, staying healthy/getting ill, and pollution. Reproduction is also covered. A teachers' resource book supported by work cards for the pupils provide very practical lessons in order to promote choice and responsibility, positive values and attitudes and the development of self-esteem. *My Body Project* has a very clear and consistent 'no smoking' message throughout.

Health Education at Key Stage 1 and Key Stage 2 (Lloyd and Morton 1992a and 1992b) offers a pragmatic and practical response to health education, approaching each of the nine components defined in Guidance 5 (NCC 1990b). They are: substance use and misuse; sex education; family life education; safety; health-related exercise; food and nutrition; personal hygiene; environmental aspects and psychological aspects. The approach is through clearly differentiated work in subjects of the National Curriculum. Accepting the importance of what pupils already know or believe, each activity is related to the nine components, e.g. Family Life, focusing on each of the core and foundation subjects, initially stating and then addressing the actual and potential relevant Programmes of Study for the Attainment Targets. As Alexander, Rose and Whitehead (1992) have pointed out previously, 'many schools have yet to make full use of National Curriculum Programmes of Study in planning topics.'

Each component is also supported by a variety of appropriate assessment activities. The activities themselves, described in the teachers' resource books and supported by photocopiable pupils' resources, develop understanding of health issues, positive attitudes to lifestyles and the skills associated with making healthy decisions.

These resources all offer teaching and learning about relationships and especially those areas which contribute to pupils' understanding of sex. However, *Knowing Me Knowing You: Strategies for Sex Education in the Primary School* (Sanders and Swindon 1990) and Lenderyou's *Primary School Work Book: Teaching Sex Education Within the National Curriculum* (1993), offer a wealth of sensitive and appropriate teaching and learning opportunities related to subjects of the National Curriculum. These emphasise the development of attitudes, skills and behaviour as well as knowledge and self awareness.

Although there is a danger of teaching health topics in isolation, smoking, alcohol, nutrition and exercise as major lifestyle issues may require individual attention in order to raise pupils' consciousness of the need for healthy behaviours. *The Dragon's Breath* (Ward 1991) for example, deals with smoking behaviours through drama, role play, music and English, whilst *We've Seen People Drinking* (Lloyd, Bennett and Lawrence 1994) offers an innovative approach to alcohol education through curriculum related activities. The latter also explores teachers' own drinking behaviour and the need for school alcohol policies. *Happy Heart* 1 and 2 (Sleap and Perch 1990, Sleap and Warburton 1990) provide the opportunity for children between the ages of 4 and 11 years to become more aware of the relationship between physical activity and health and to become more active generally.

The value of encouraging healthy eating through appropriate strategies in schools cannot be understated. The contribution of the Schools Nutrition Action Groups (Harvey & Passmore, 1994) is important to the development of policies for managing food and nutrition in schools.

Conclusion

In developing health education within the curriculum, primary schools must avoid contriving to make links where they are at most tenuous or do not fit at all. At stake is the integrity of individual subjects. Alexander, Rose and Whitehead (1992) recommend a 'subject focused' topic approach which may also include aspects of other relevant subjects, in that this will 'provide more opportunity for the sequential development of pupils' knowledge, understanding and skills.'

This has to be as true for health education as it is for subjects of the National Curriculum. Moreover, those involved in teaching and learning for health education are recommended to consider the 'factors associated with best classroom practice' (OFSTED 1993) which emphasise the importance of organisational strategies, teaching techniques and teachers' knowledge, which are similarly just as appropriate to health education as to any other curriculum area.

As a topic health education should be at the centre of the curriculum. To say that there is not enough time in the week, the month, the term or indeed the school year is to diminish the concept of the health-promoting primary school. It was never the intention that the National Curriculum should occupy the whole of school time, a point made by Dearing (1993), who recommends that 'a margin (of time) for use by the school is needed in the interests of providing the best possible education.'

Education is not only concerned with examinations, qualifications and future employment. As Dearing further argues,

> It must help our young people to: use leisure time creatively; have respect for other people, other cultures and other beliefs; become good citizens; think things out for themselves; pursue a healthy lifestyle; and, not least, value themselves and their achievements.

If we accept Wragg's (1991) premise that 'the nation's future well-being is at stake', then the curriculum of the health-promoting primary school should be at the heart of this process, and as he comments, 'think of all those attainment targets just waiting to be ticked off.'

However, health curriculum in the context of the health-promoting primary school should be worth doing for its own sake; informing, involving and inspiring pupils; building upon their knowledge and beliefs; raising self-esteem and self concept and promoting effective, independent learning.

CHAPTER 10
Reviewing, Monitoring, Evaluation and Inspection

Muriel Phillingham

Introduction

A health-promoting school does not materialise as a happy accident. Any school may have aspects within it that are health-promoting, and that is creditable. But an unplanned approach produces incoherence, omissions and contradictions. It is, therefore, essential that health promotion, both within and beyond the curriculum, is planned for, regularly reviewed for its effectiveness, monitored as to its implementation, and, within inspection, overtly accountable to its community.

The Education Reform Act 1988 requires those who manage a school to provide 'a balanced and broadly based curriculum which: a) promotes the spiritual, moral, cultural, mental and physical development of pupils and of society; and b) prepares such pupils for the opportunities, responsibilities and experience of adult life.'

The White Paper of 1992, *Choice and Diversity: A new framework for schools*, identifies, 'Imperatives for the 1990s'. These include the need for constant review of 'the moral dimension of a school', the development of a 'good school ethos' and 'regularly investigating how schools are getting on' by means of inspection. Whereas the moral dimension is quite properly related to religious education, 'the spiritual, cultural, mental and physical development of boys and girls as part of preparing them for adult life' also has strong resonances with personal, social and health education. The connection is enhanced in the expectation that children should be encouraged to appreciate 'the needs of others and their environment'.

Such aspirations need to be more than high-sounding phrases. They imply that the school has policies to provide guidance and a structure for analysis, dissemination, implementation and evaluation. The question that arises is 'How might all this be managed?' We have the substantial and dauntingly documented National Curriculum and the local structures for religious education which together comprise the statutory requirements of the taught curriculum. These must be the starting point for implementing the broad aspirations of the Act and the aims which the school has set for itself.

Managing The Curriculum

Curriculum management within school is a complex task. It depends on the development of a whole school framework which maps out subject content together with methods of approach and assessment. It is, therefore, vital that both overview and detailed planning are given sufficient support to cut out wearisome, repetitive writing. Prepared pages which have a consistent structure can give teachers such support. Many appropriate proforma have been developed.

Much emphasis has inevitably been given since the 1988 Education Reform Act to the familiarisation with and establishment of schemes of work in conformity with the statutory orders for the core and other foundation subjects as they became available. Health Education and its companion themes have consequently been given less attention than many teachers would wish and less than that which the well-being of children needs and deserves. Now that the structure and content of the core and foundation subjects have become more familiar, the two main methods of curriculum planning at primary level need to include the consideration of cross-curricular issues. The basic curriculum must include the core and other foundation subjects plus religious education. These are to be 'set in the context of the whole curriculum' by policies to employ a range of dimensions, one of which is personal and social education. This 'is defined to include cross-curricular themes such as health education'. These dimensions should be woven throughout the life and work of the school, in every area of the curriculum, and be addressed by every teacher. It is essential that there is a common school viewpoint which will guarantee a consistent approach. (NCC 1989)

Formal school inspection gives encouragement, since it is expected that proper consideration will be given to the inclusion of these dimensions. An OFSTED report routinely includes a section on 'Pupils' personal development and behaviour' and, within the general points about the quality and range of the curriculum, might include a statement such as, 'A broad range of cross-curricular themes is provided including health education and environmental education' OFSTED (1993). Press publicity in early 1994 for OFSTED adds further pressure as we are told that 'Personal development cannot be hived off into...such activities as assemblies...or classes in religious, personal or social education.' The press comment which follows the OFSTED report puts responsibility firmly in the realm of health education – 'Most teenagers relied on the media for information about sex, drugs and AIDS...' (*Daily Telegraph,* 26 February 1994).

Material from the themes can provide the links and coherence that help children to make connections between subjects which have no apparent common ground. Some of us were taught as students that it is this ability to make connections which marks out those who are intelligent! The model which comes to mind is from the world of textiles (Figure 10.1).

The continuous threads through the length of woven cloth are like the subjects running through the continuing process of education. Some threads may cease and others be tied in, but the warp runs throughout. However, although there is at this stage both a structure and a pattern, the strength and completion of the pattern only comes from the introduction of the weft threads that are woven across the warp. So it is with the cross-curricular themes. They complete the pattern and strengthen the understanding of concepts and issues across the range of subjects.

Some suggestions are given below in Figures 10.2, 10.3 (MEP 1993) and 10.4 of examples of proforma with which to focus attention on and encourage a balanced approach to all the cross curricular themes. As befits the title of this book, these examples focus on health education.

Subjects Named and Timetabled Slots

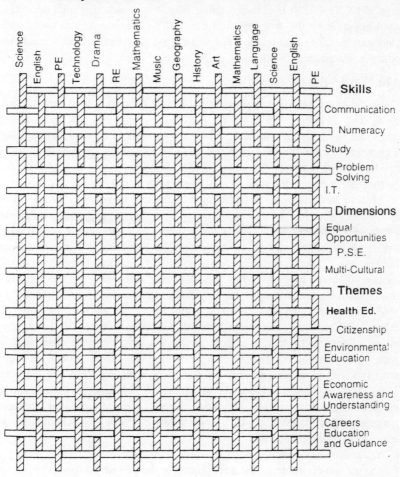

The curriculum which we offer our young people should contain all the threads, formal, informal and hidden, and should be like the fabric: strong, serviceable, balanced and fit for the purpose.

Figure 10.1 The Tartan Curriculum Model

Planning

Primary schools use one of the two main methods for planning the curriculum, based either on a topic or on the delivery of the individual subjects, and sometimes adopt an amalgam of the two, as for example in the subject focused topic, commended as 'an efficient way forward.' (Alexander, Rose and Whitehead, 1992). It is the prerogative of the school and its community of parents and governors to make that choice. 'It is not appropriate, or desirable, in Council's view that all primary schools should follow the same pattern of curriculum organisation.' NCC (1989). It is at the planning stage that monitoring and, later, review must begin, since the weaving in of the health education weft threads needs to coincide with the range and level of work previously determined in the school's policy and scheme of work.

The Topic-Based Approach

The topic-based approach to planning within the primary school curriculum proceeds with an overview planned for a term or series of weeks, and it is at this stage that the relevant cross-curricular themes need to be identified. It may be appropriate to have a dominant theme and also to include some material relevant to other themes within any one topic, and to give prominence to a different theme on the next occasion. On such a basis all the themes would receive due attention. So health education might naturally be a dominant theme for a topic on 'Water', be used as a supporting theme within a topic on 'Movement' and, for the sake of a balanced approach, not feature in the planning for a topic on 'Toys'. The omission of health education from the topic would *not* be because it has no relevance, but because it is important to introduce and ensure reasonable coverage of all the themes and avoid repetition. It is, actually, quite difficult to find no relevance to health education in any topic! Equally there are occasions when the topic itself might be centred around health education. Many schools use the topic 'Ourselves' and inevitably cover much health education material. The danger is to allow a haphazard selection of content to meet only the immediate needs of a topic. 'The intrinsic complexity of topic work means that problems will remain until rigorous planning becomes the norm.' (Alexander, Rose and Whitehead, 1992). Unless the school has a planned approach, a balance of themes and their content becomes impossible. Therefore, the allocation of cross-curricular theme material should increasingly be a normal part of the whole school curriculum framework planning process.

At the overview planning stage it is easy to identify the relevant themes in relation to the subject content, select and highlight the one which should be dominant and decide whether another should also receive consideration. Review will address balance and the subsequent revision help to secure the place for each theme within the whole school curriculum framework. Health education thus becomes part of a planned structure to meet the needs of the children. It receives due consideration from the start and benefits from being a natural part of the topic material. The consequent identification of needs for staff development in health education is then a normal part of the school's curriculum development and evaluation. Figure 10.2 gives an example of a proforma which would support the overview planning for a topic and encourage the identification of cross-curricular theme material.

The Subject-Based Approach

The subject-based approach is the other main method of curriculum management, often based on term by term allocations of subject content. The selection of cross curricular theme material within planning may be more diverse and varied than in topic planning. Theme material would be selected to be specifically related to the content of individual subjects. So health education may contribute significantly to the work within the one and different themes be employed in conjunction with the other subjects in the same term. The whole school framework for curriculum management plays an equally important role and great care is required to ensure balance and coverage of all themes. There is, nevertheless, a strong likelihood that current events or the choice of subject content for a term will naturally create a subject-focused topic, or the circumstances of the school will give rise to some grouping together of content. The theme material that is relevant to the individual subjects would then become less dissimilar. Since the selection of theme material to be woven into the subject can be independent of that selected for any other subject, it may be somewhat easier to plan the delivery of health education content at the appropriate level. A proforma to support planning for a period of time, maybe for a term, would not be unlike Figure 10.2, as may be seen from Figure 10.3.

Short-term planning forms for each way of working are a useful extension and using them at A3 size makes their completion easier. These would naturally be used by teachers for planning a week's work and some may then find this type of sheet useful for daily planning, including the identification of assessment experiences. Certainly such proforma should be seen as useful only if they reduce the amount of repetitive writing by providing headed areas on the page and by placing subject specific material in predictable sites on each page. Part-time and supply teachers could also be the beneficiaries from a structure which gives them easily accessible information. Figures 10.2a and 10.3a illustrate such an adaptation from long term to short term planning.

Both methods of curriculum management have their strengths and weaknesses within primary education. The vital point is that the curriculum is well managed within both subjects and topics, and that the cross curricular themes are carefully planned to strengthen and give coherence to the programme of work.

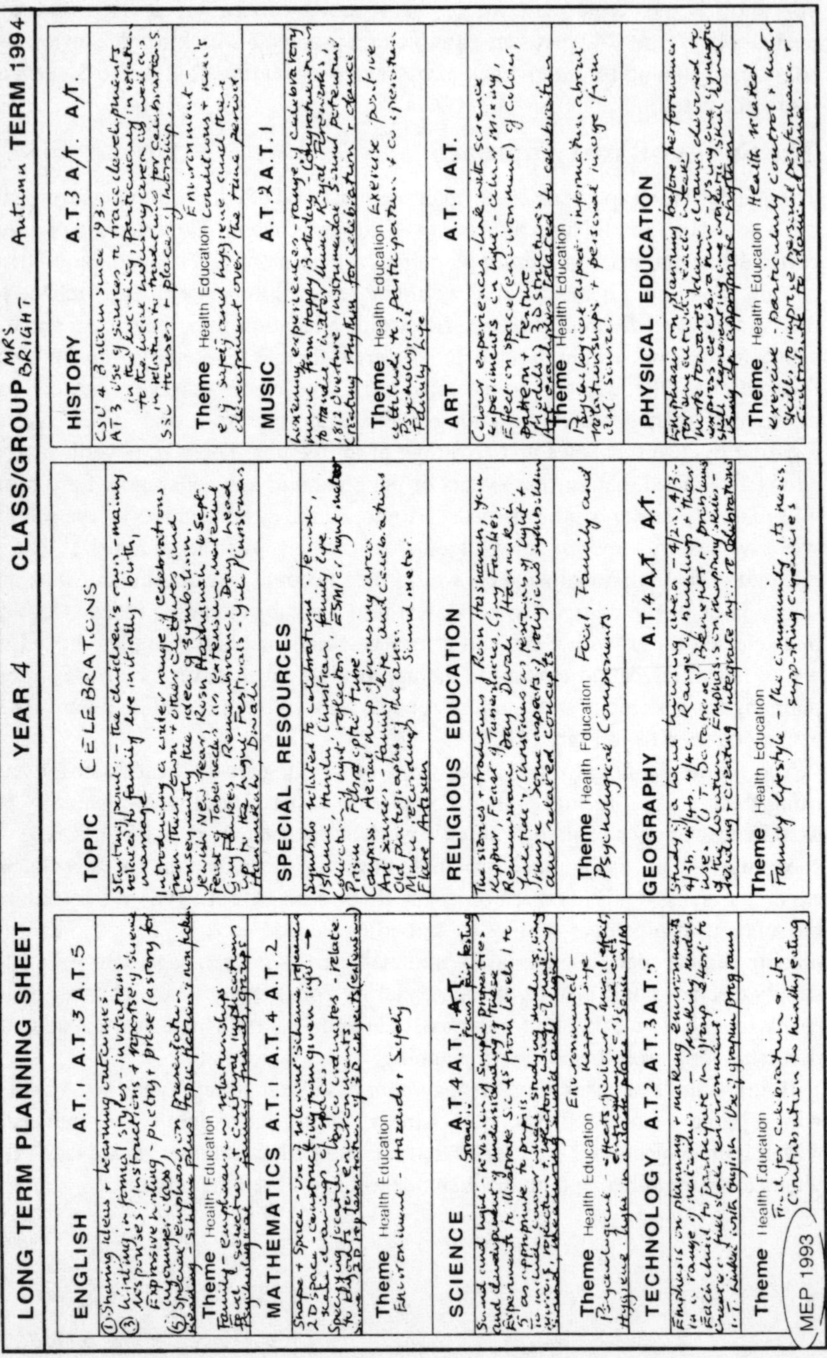

LONG TERM PLANNING SHEET — YEAR 4 — CLASS/GROUP MRS BRIGHT — Autumn TERM 1994

ENGLISH A.T.1 A.T.3 A.T.5

(1) Sharing ideas + learning outcomes.
(3) Writing in formal styles - invitations responses; instructions + reports e.g. science. Expressive writing - poetry + prose (a story for a younger class)
(5) Special emphasis on presentation
Reading - scheme plus topic fiction + non fiction

Theme Health Education
Family - emphasis on relationships
Food - selection + cultural implications
Psychological - family, friends, groups

MATHEMATICS A.T.1 A.T.4 A.T.2

Shape + Space - use of relevant scheme references
2D space - constructing from given info → scale drawings of spaces.
Specifying location by co ordinates - relate to projects for environments.
Some 2D representation of 3D objects (extension)

Theme Health Education
Environment - Hazards + Safety

SCIENCE A.T.4 A.T.1 A.T.

Strand ii / focus fair testing
Sound and light - revision of simple properties and development of understanding of these
Experiments to illustrate S.C 4s from levels 1 to 5 as appropriate to pupils.
To include colour shade, studying shadows, using mirrors, reflection + reflectors, using + making sound, measuring sound and light

Theme Health Education
Psychological - effects of colour - mood effect; Environmental - keeping safe
Hygiene - light in a classroom; environment c.f. sound; Sense of/M

TECHNOLOGY A.T.2 A.T.3 A.T.5

Emphasis on planning + making environments in a range of materials - making models
Each child to participate in group effort to create a full scale environment.
I.T. linked with English - use of graphic programs

Theme Health Education
Food for celebration + its contribution to healthy eating

TOPIC CELEBRATIONS

Starting point: - the children's own - mainly related to family life initially - birth, marriage
Introducing a wider range of celebrations from their own + other cultures and consequently the idea of symbolism.
Jewish New Year, Rosh Hashanah - 6 Sept.
Feast of Tabernacles as extension material
Guy Fawkes, Remembrance Day. Lead up to the light Festivals - Yule / Christmas Hannukah, Diwali

SPECIAL RESOURCES

Symbols related to celebrations - Jewish, Islamic, Hindu, Christian, family life
Collection of light reflectors. ESM/Cr light meter
Prism Fibre optic tube.
Compass. Aerial map of housing area.
Art sources - family life and celebrations
Old photographs of the area.
Music recordings Sound meter
Flare, Artesian

RELIGIOUS EDUCATION

The stories + traditions of Rosh Hashanah, Yom Kippur, Feast of Tabernacles, Guy Fawkes, Remembrance Day, Diwali, Hannukah, Fireworks, Christmas as festivals of light + music. Some aspects of religious symbolism and related concepts

Theme Health Education Food, Family and Psychological Components.

GEOGRAPHY A.T.4 A.T. A.T.

Study of a local housing area - 4/2a, 4/3a, 4/3b, 4/4b, 4/4c. Range of buildings + their uses. (I.T. Database) Benefits + problems of the location. Emphasis on mapping skills - locating + creating. Integrate in re celebrations

Theme Health Education
Family lifestyle - the community, its needs, supporting agencies

HISTORY A.T.3 A/T. A/T.

CSU 4 Britain since 1930
AT3 Use of sources to trace developments in the locality, particularly in relation to the local housing area as well as in relation to traditions for celebrations.
SSU Houses + places of worship.

Theme Health Education Environment - conditions + needs e.g. safety and hygiene and their development over the time period.

MUSIC A.T.2 A.T.1

Listening experiences - range of celebratory music from Happy Birthday - Congratulations to Handel - Water Music, Royal Fireworks, 1812 Overture. Instrumental sound potential
Creating rhythm for celebration + dance

Theme Health Education Exercise positive attitude to participation + co operation
Psychological
Family life

ART A.T.1 A.T.

Colour experiences - link with science experiments on light - colour mixing, Effect on space (environment) of colour, pattern + texture.
Models of 3D structures
Art examples related to celebrations

Theme Health Education
Psychological aspect - information about relationships + personal image from art sources

PHYSICAL EDUCATION

Emphasis on planning before performance for one activity each week.
Work towards dance drama devised to express celebration - using one gymnastic skill representing one athletic skill and using an appropriate rhythm

Theme Health Education Health related exercise - particularly control + motor skills, to improve personal performance + contribute to dance drama

MEP 1993

FIGURE 10.2 Topic-based Planning Sheet

SHORT TERM PLANNING SHEET   YEAR 4   CLASS/GROUP Mrs BRENT   WEEK ENDING 21/10/94

TOPIC CELEBRATIONS   Week 7

ENGLISH   S.O.As 1/2c, 1/3e, 5/3, 2/2b, 3/3b, 3/2
1. Showing class for mystery celebration in groups. Reading scheme books.
2. Handwriting for the week - surveying, for e.g. different styles. Group reporting on skills and vocabulary.
3. Educational visit to cinema. Prog. plan vocabulary about topic related to visit to Paris.

Theme Health Education   Psychological - group interaction reviewed

MATHEMATICS S.O.As 4/3c, 4/4b 4/4d
Maths Scheme - continue work on decimal place. Prepare to plan for the celebration on either a picnic for the whole group with compass point or literature to investigate & find the student nature. Use instruction to find the mystery location.

Theme Health Education —

SCIENCE   S.O.As 4/4/1c, 3d, 5e focus
Experiments with light to see the effects of colour mixing & create change. Extension note - measuring light intensity/filters to add, carry investigation. Effects on colour of reflecting light.

Theme Health Education   Safety - responsibility for self + others to hazards from behaviour & report   Psychological experience

TECHNOLOGY S.O.As 1/2c, 1/3b 1/4c 2/2c, 2/3, 4/3c 4/4
Media environment. Celebration after half term. Group work. Features to create the atmosphere. Includes Technology potential enquiry to do one theme... Technology everyone use.

Theme Health Education   Safety - responsibility for self & others. First - healthy eating for a cold night.

RESOURCES
Squared and graph paper. ESM or light meter. Lamp holder & different wattage bulbs.
Coloured paper & colour acetates. Suitable boxes for light experiments. Examples: formula instructions & travel instruction - from context to mainstream to prose (descriptive style)

RELIGIOUS EDUCATION
Story of Guy Fawkes. The facts about Gunpowder and Filling. Ask - Why is the story distorted? Factual reporting/biased an account to various versions. The moral dilemma - was the punishment just? Compare. The facts important/easy to recreate purpose whole activity through whole experience

Theme Health Education   Safety - taking responsibility for self & direct others

GEOGRAPHY   S.O.As 4/10, 4/1b 4/2a, 4/2b
Using local maps to prepare location plan and directions for finding the mystery celebration venue in relation to the local environment. Study work over the distance for the whole term note.

Theme Health Education   Environmental hazards   Psychological - friendships & loyalty within group with common interest

HISTORY   S.O.As
Second world war experience - life writing. Relate - blackout. Why & how was it done? Relate to local. Building a try to find how they did it. People's experience. The blackout - effects on life style - Did they have to modify their own circumstance?

Theme Health Education   Safety - self protection   Psychological - group formation, friendship and loyalty

MUSIC   S.O.As 2/1 2/1 2/v
Listen to & select music for the mystery celebration. Can music create a mood/atmosphere. Using instruments, find sounds that express - patter, pace, rhythm & crescendo. First hearing - The Royal Fireworks.

Theme Health Education
Family life - empathy & communication

ART   S.O.As KS2 - 1/v, 1/vii 1/viii
Colour mixing with print. Compare results with science work. Work with one colour only to produce different effects - a repeating pattern, a shadow abstract, a textured surface, a plain surface - use to make environment about.
Psychological - how best know you feel? Is one colour adequate? Emotional response

Theme Health Education
Family life

PHYSICAL EDUCATION KS2 c,ii *
Planning emphasis - developing/turning movements to develop individual personal skill through games, gymnastics & swimming. Group work selecting the gymnastic skills. The dance through & beginning techniques for... sequences.

Theme Health Education   Health - natural exercise - co-operative attitude to dance & movement. Plus development of dance experience & motor skills.

MEP 1993

LONG TERM PLANNING SHEET   YEAR 4   CLASS/GROUP Mr Shepherd   Autumn TERM 1994

ENGLISH   A.T.1 A.T.2 A.T.3

① Speaking & listening - giving & responding to instructions. - reporting observations

③ Writing - instructions & reports - use of appropriate styles - extended writing - story about a Victorian child in the area.

② Reading - using scheme & cultural and reading tricks and emphasis on information retrieval skills.

Theme Health Education
Safety of self and others in the activities considered

MATHEMATICS A.T.2 A.T.4 A.T.1

2/3st + 2/4th Estimate and check measurement eg mass & measure eic wty of hime around school & measure the measurement 4/2a, 4/4a, 4/5a, 4/5d wt use
the accurate area of cubic capacity of brick 4/3c 4/4b location
diagram area & relevant sections from maths scheme.

Theme Health Education

SCIENCE   A.T.3 A.T.1 A.T.

3/1a, 3/1n 6 Experiment to explore the properties of a range of materials & show ways in which they can be made to change.
A.T.1 Predicting & observing accurately.
Different methods of recording observations. Different methods of recording observations — Link with English AT3

Theme Health Education
Safety for any & others in the experiment. Safety of the procedure & of substance
Misuse of effects in the environment.

MEP 1993

SPECIAL POINTS/EVENTS/RESOURCES

Starting point ideas for activities which require instructions. Surveying books for examples of different styles.
Ot Photographs of the area.
Aerial + thematic scale maps of the area.
Wall calendars - living
Book week - Cultural + recording graph etc
Assignments

TECHNOLOGY A.T.1 A.T.2 A.T.3

Identification of needs for healthy snacks and treasured possibilities
Emphasis on design for play time
- A healthy snack for play time
- A drive to sell in the school tuckshop
- Design for a container for a specially treasured item or house or school

Theme Health Education Food + Nutrition
Economic Awareness

RELIGIOUS EDUCATION

From curricular notes - The Church's Year.
Jewish Single chapter's issue Jewish feasts.
Understanding of festivals significance + stories
What people do, many feelings. The function
of symbols

Theme Health Education Food + Culture
Citizenship - a pluralist society

GEOGRAPHY   A.T.   A.T.   A.T.

The local area - Environment + Eca
The resources - The acquisition/employment
and town effects. Field trip. p.234
Using different types of local maps
Creating simple maps link identified pictures

Theme Health Education Safety
Citizenship - the citizen & the law

HISTORY   A.T.1 A.T.2 A.T.3

CSC 3 victorians + the local area.
SSC Houses + places of worship.

Theme Health Education Family + Hygiene
Citizenship - public services eg gas eg
- Family lifestyle

MUSIC   A.T.2 A.T.

2a Listening to a range of composed works
of different styles.
1f introducing instruments to try similar
activities - choose from pitch, instrumental
sound to create other various range's.

Theme Health Education Psychological Asp

ART   A.T.1 A.T.

P.C 1, 11, v.
Observational drawing around school.
Doing a sketch book in a school visit
Exploring the use of media - paint, pastels
and children

Theme Health Education Safety - hazard
identification and allergy -

PHYSICAL EDUCATION.

Develop ball skills for football + netball
Gymnastics - emphases in rolling + balancing
Work on a 3 movement sequence chain using

Theme Health Education Health Related
exercise - physical activity - energy
use + need - control + motor skills

FIGURE 10.3 Subject-based Planning Sheet

SHORT TERM PLANNING SHEET YEAR 4 CLASS/GROUP Mr. Shepherd WEEK ENDING 21/10/—

ENGLISH S.O.As 1/3/2c, 3d, 3b

A.T.
① Give precise instructions for chosen activity.
② Developing an information search within maths.
— make a note taking web.
Assessments from reading science.
③ Writing instructions — some numeracy for different recipient.
Providing a note well to keep class informed throughout display.

Theme Health Education
1 T Prediction

MATHEMATICS S.O.As 4/2a 4/3a 4/4c 4/4d

Working with measures —
Scheme material related to measures.
Construct 2D & 3D shapes.
2D — find perimeters of rectangles.
Apply practical calculations.
Using practical/paper Measuring data to drawing.

Theme Health Education

SCIENCE S.O.As AT1 Producing AT3 Textiles

Strands 3/1a & 3/4b
accuracy of observation chart making.
To record observations significance in how to full task in — link with English.
Textiles — Decide what we want to know — course relevant tests & identifying criteria. Specific enquiry. To incorporate location/direction & sense of risk.

Theme Health Education Effects for self & others. Effects on the immediate environment.

MEP 1993

SPECIAL POINTS/EVENTS/RESOURCES

Graph paper.
Old photographs of the area.
Speech bubbles prepared.
Think first trip ideas.
Copy of Mrs Beeton & Elizabeth David's Cookery bks.
Assessments essential.

TECHNOLOGY S.O.As AT1/2c 3a, 3h AT1, 2a 3, 3b, 3c

Design a clause to be sold in the school workshop in the winter. Design what container it will be in and how it will be promoted.

Theme Health Education Food & Nutrition. Economic Awareness. Marketing, cost, outcome.

RELIGIOUS EDUCATION

All Hallows' Evening — colour with the celebration about how they had their celebration. Old & Compare reading number than we do. Old & Compare The Christmas wish, introduce topics & other religious beliefs in what they want in the world. Is there any human in Halloween etc.

Theme Health Education Psychological — respect for others feelings & emotions.

GEOGRAPHY S.O.As 1/2b, 3c.

Create your own maps of a very simple area. Carried about house. Living together in a Civic. Identify significance & features.

Theme Health Education Environmental — Environmental Education.

HISTORY S.O.As 1/3a 1/3b

Groupwork team — Describe a change made in since Victorian times in the area. Make a display re Victorian Era building & space. Make & display the household and past present for change in space business until a present. Each group to work with different space/building.

Theme Health Education Hygiene.

MUSIC S.O.As 2i, 2ii, 2iv 2v

Listen to the Carnival of the Animals — identify the animals sounds and other instruments & sounds. Instruments are used.

Theme Health Education Psychological — group music.

ART S.O.As KS.2 1/i, 1/iii

Observational drawing — first hand around the locality of a sketch look. Use several bks & sources to illustrate. Grey, field and explore the use of pastels.

Theme Health Education

PHYSICAL EDUCATION

KS 2 Games SCA ii Ball skills
Gymnastics — explore & demonstrate a balance showing the development. Practice — sequence to decide on a sequence.

Theme Health Education Control & motor skill. Health, Rest, Exercise. Strength suppleness.

FIGURE 10.3a Short-term Subject-based Planning Sheet

Teaching Methods

All the areas of health education are of vital importance to the well-being of children both in day to day living at the present time and as preparation for informed decision making as they grow up. They are continuously surrounded by enticements to make choices and to act in ways that are not health-promoting. They need skills and information to guide them. This must inevitably influence the methods of learning selected for them. In days when 'chalk and talk' is strongly promoted as *the* method of imparting information, it is important to remember that everyone has their own best way of learning. Perhaps our own most recent learning experience will inform as to the selection of learning activities for children. Certainly there was no substitute for hands on activity in getting to grips with the National Curriculum! Those early days of finding to which page of which file familiar material had been allocated, or the discovery of some new demands – and then what was expected for children to demonstrate achievement – will long remain in the memory of those involved. We all had to put ourselves on a fast learning curve and the only effective way was activity based – to *do* something about it oneself! It is from that experience that primary teachers now know so much of the content of the Attainments Targets and the levels of the Statements of Attainment by heart. It is doubtful whether any set out to learn them by rote!

Good teachers, of course, employ a range of methods, suiting their selection to the material being presented and the learning needs of the children. Good teachers know a great deal about their pupils, but even the best get some surprises. One memorable example comes from the use of the 'Draw and Write' technique used to survey how much Key Stage 1 children already know about *'What makes and keeps you healthy'* (Williams, Wetton and Moon, 1989). Certainly the learning methods should be those which engage the children in active learning experiences, designed to affect behaviour and engage their commitment to the health education messages being presented. Indeed, *Curriculum Guidance 3; The Whole Curriculum* (NCC 1990a) makes the point that 'the very teaching methods deployed...make an important contribution to personal and social education...' 'Opportunities should be provided for pupils to assess evidence, make decisions, negotiate, listen, make and deal with relationships, solve problems and work independently and with confidence.' (NCC 1990b).

Assessment

The selected learning methods often lead naturally to appropriate methods of assessment. This is a word which is sometimes a worry to those who are concerned with health education. 'Assessment' brings with it connotations of formal tests and examinations. There may, of course, be times when a written test to check on factual knowledge seems quite appropriate, but often other methods will be more suited to the subject matter and in themselves provide further opportunities to reinforce the learning. Sometimes the products of the children's work are eloquent testimony to their grasp of the principles they have learned. At other times they might be asked to share what they have learned for the benefit of others as a talk, investigation, display or promotion. The methods of assessment of children's understanding are many and varied. Methods which reveal whether children have changed behaviour or reinforced healthy lifestyles are ultimately more worthwhile. The examples of teaching methods 'particularly suited...'include:

> games, simulations, case studies, role plays, problem solving exercises, questionnaires, surveys, open-ended questions and sentences and group work. All offer good opportunities to assess children's understanding of the health education concepts with which they have been working. NCC(1990b)

> Continuous assessment by teachers should be based on a range of activities and outcomes, the assessment technique depending on the activity being undertaken. NCC(1989)

It is important that children realise that their work is being appropriately assessed and given status and value. Without this a good deal of what has been done might readily be cancelled out, because the children may be left with the impression that those who are responsible for their learning do not deem this work as sufficiently important to give it due recognition and respect. If that is important for the foundation subjects, how much it must be so in relation to learning about health!

> One obvious aspect of assessment which needs emphasis is that pupils need genuine feedback about the success or otherwise of their learning. The evidence suggests that while pupils are generally clear about what they have to do, they often do not receive enough information about the purposes of their learning and, what is even more important, how well they are doing. (Alexander, Rose and Whitehead, 1992)

'Assessment is at the heart of the process of promoting children's learning.' DES (1988). It is not a question of testing for pass or failure in healthy behaviour. It is, rather, the use of strategies which enable children to see for themselves or reveal how much they have understood of the principles on which their work has centred and to what extent they wish to live out the healthy behaviour which has been commended to them. Strategies such as improvised drama, involvement in planning for future learning, designing promotions for their peers or writing stories for younger children and the involvement of health considerations in designing for a given situation, e.g. a new uniform for a police officer, work well in revealing how much children have absorbed. There are times when the pressure that they exert on their parents to support healthy behaviour will also be telling evidence of how work in school has had a real influence on their attitudes! This last point, of course, serves to emphasise the importance of having the support of the school's community for the health education policy and scheme of work, as well as illustrating how school-based education may actually influence today's adult society. Valid assessment depends on referring back to the initial purpose of the work. So, whether the assessment is made by the children themselves about their understanding, whether by their peers in a carefully planned adjudication or by their teachers, it must be in relation to those initial objectives for the 'package' to work. To serve their purpose fully, those objectives must be checkable by appropriate methods.

The outcome of assessment is an essential tool for review and evaluation. Work which has engaged the commitment of the children, allowed the achievement of high quality work, or positively affected behaviour is worthy of being maintained and encouraged. If the reverse is true, both the selection of content and the teaching methods need serious reconsideration and modification.

Monitoring

Primary schools have increasingly shared the responsibility for curriculum management and monitoring amongst staff. This has encouraged interdependence and made coping with the workload a little easier. As with the subjects, the role of co-ordinator for health education is crucial (HMI 1986, NCC 1990b). Supporting, resourcing and monitoring the health education programme in school cannot be successful on piecemeal basis. Someone has to have the overview and ensure that all children receive the health education programme which they need and to which they are entitled. Having been instrumental in producing the health education scheme of work in association with the whole school curriculum framework, the co-ordinator needs to be informed about the health education that colleagues both plan to and actually include. Here again the benefits of proforma which make monitoring as easy as possible will be appreciated. The co-ordinator has the responsibility of checking that the range of health education has been covered within appropriate key stages.

The grid principle for checking is helpful since it readily shows what has been done, can be used to discourage repetition and is eloquent witness to material that has been omitted. The grids in *Curriculum Guidance 5* section 5, are a useful model to chart the implementation of the school's health education scheme of work. With top headings which list the detail of the areas of substance misuse, sex education, family life education, etc, allocated to a year group, by the end of the summer term that year group's grid should be complete. If it is *not*, the review process is made easier and the complex task of the co-ordinator somewhat more realistic. At the same time, the school is engaged in a genuine audit of what is being done, rather than the idealistic aspirations of 'what might be done if the subject crops up'.

Review, evaluation and monitoring ultimately depend on asking those questions which will reveal whether planning, implementing, control over and subsequent reflection on what has been done have all taken place. However, it is not just a matter of 'Has it been done?' 'Can we count it to tick it off?' That quantitative element of evaluation is important and must feature as part of our accountability. Equally, the quality of the work must also be questioned. Has the work been worthwhile and effective? Have the children acquired new skills which support them in developing and maintaining a healthy lifestyle? How do we know? Does the normal conduct of the school support the aims and objectives of the health education policy or is it a question of – 'What you *are* is shouting so loud that I can't hear what you are saying!?'

Evaluation needs to be focused to be of maximum worth. It is important to identify who the evaluation is for, what area is to be concentrated on and what outcome is intended. This last point leads naturally to the formation of an action plan to strengthen and modify the planning for the future. Many schools would see the evaluation of the taught curriculum as their prime focus, for the purpose of its refinement and to meet the needs of both teachers and pupils. Others may feel that there is a need to know the aspirations and concerns of the school's community and evaluate whether the 'hidden curriculum' of the school's lifestyle supports or confirms these. There is much value in being overtly accountable to the local community, not merely because we should, but because it draws out the support of those who have an interest in the school and that is probably the best reinforcement to the children's learning for which we could wish. Whatever the focus of such an action plan, this then takes its place within the whole school development plan.

Best practice would no doubt come from each school designing its own schedule of questions by which to judge performance. But this is a time-consuming task and the examples of questions in the grid on Figure 10.4 may form a useful starting point for self-assessment as to whether the school may be justly described as health-promoting.

The life style of each school is made up from:

● The Formal Curriculum – that which is included in the curriculum framework;
● The Informal Curriculum – that which is included in the extra curricular activities;
● The 'Hidden Curriculum' – that which is lived out in the daily conduct of the school.

All these aspects of school life have to be planned, put into effect, monitored or controlled and reviewed and possibly modified. Figure 10.4 offers a schematic approach to encourage consideration of all three aspects. These questions allow consideration of the taught curriculum, the range of activities of the school and all aspects of its lifestyle to see whether each supports the health education policy. This consideration needs to be given in relation to planning, implementing, monitoring or controlling and evaluating, both as activities proceed and in retrospect. 'Does health education feature?' and 'Is the contribution worthwhile?' would serve to sum up the questions with quantitative and qualitative emphasis respectively. Both emphases are important. Formal school inspection may often seem to give more attention to the quantitative type of question and this is important for the purpose of accountability. However, the most difficult questions, both to ask and to answer, focus on the quality and effectiveness of what is done. Ultimately these qualitative questions will prove to be those which are most important in the education and development of the children. To illustrate the point, take the sample questions from Figure 10.4 relating to the Delivering of the Formal Curriculum:

	FORMAL	INFORMAL	HIDDEN
PLANNING	QUALITATIVE: Is there a planned progression through the phase / Key Stage? Is health education integral in short term planning? QUANTITATIVE: Are there health education objectives identified for many of the 'packages'?	QUALITATIVE: Is there planned support for the health education programme within the informal lifestyle of the school? QUANTITATIVE: Is there genuine planning in health education considerations?	QUALITATIVE: Is there planning, supportive of health education, related to the conduct of the lifestyle of the school? QUANTITATIVE: Is the lifestyle of the school positively intended to support its health education policy?
DELIVERING	QUALITATIVE: Is the allocated element actually included in the delivery? QUANTITATIVE: Does the conduct / methodology support the objective(s) of the 'package'?	QUALITATIVE: Are there actual and evident examples of implementation of the health education philosophy as planned? QUANTITATIVE: Is there evidence of pupils' contributions, capabilities and strengths being overtly valued across the full spectrum of school life?	QUALITATIVE: Are there examples in the lifestyle of the school which support or undermine the health education policy? QUANTITATIVE: Are there examples of behaviour which supports or undermines the health education policy?
MONITORING	QUALITATIVE: Are the planning and delivery of the progression monitored and recorded? QUANTITATIVE: Is the monitoring slick, therefore maintained and used as a tool for planning / modification, therefore effective?	QUALITATIVE: Is there a range of health education considerations related to the planned progression? QUANTITATIVE: Is there evidence of awareness of the contribution that the current activity / event can make to the planned progression?	QUALITATIVE: Is there positive action to raise awareness and modify the school's lifestyle to support health education? QUANTITATIVE: Are there opportunities for identifying behaviour in the lifestyle of the school which supports / undermines the health education policy?
EVALUATING	QUALITATIVE: Are there occasions when consideration of effectiveness / needs for modification are carried out? QUANTITATIVE: Are there agreed criteria to serve as a basis for evaluation, used to inform assessment procedures?	QUALITATIVE: Is the contribution to health education part of the evaluation of the process / activity / event? QUANTITATIVE: Do the criteria for evaluation recognise the health education needs and opportunities?	QUALITATIVE: Are there occasions when the principles of the health education policy are used to evaluate the school's lifestyle? QUANTITATIVE: Are the personnel encouraged to analyse the lifestyle of the school to evaluate its support for the health education policy?

Figure 10.4 Evaluation Questions for Health Education

Quantitative – Is the allocated element (i.e. from the scheme of work) actually included in the delivery?

This is readily dealt with by a yes/no answer and is useful information for teacher, co-ordinator, head teacher, parent or governor. It is an essential tool for monitoring that what has been agreed is actually being carried out. It can be seen as straightforward accountability.

Qualitative – Does the conduct/methodology support the objective(s) of the 'package'?

The scheme of work is presumed to have identified aims relevant to the progressing phases of the work, through the key stage, from which the learning objectives would be derived. The learning experiences which are presented to the children need to support those purposes identified for this small section (the 'package') of work selected from the whole scheme. It is, of course, the principle of 'fitness for purpose' which should underpin all that we do in education. A response to either of these questions could find a place in the inspection framework's lesson observation proforma under the heading of 'Contribution to Achievement in Other Areas' or in 'Factors Contributing to these Findings' and so play its part in a wider sphere of accountability (OFSTED 1993 Part 7 para. 7.1.1 and 7.1.3.) But how much better to get the credit for having thought about it beforehand.

It is important to have agreement within the staff team, both teaching and non-teaching, that the whole lifestyle of the school will positively support the health education policy. It means, of course, that all must be aware of the policy and actively guard its aims in every aspect of school life. It also means that parents and regular visitors, particularly those who may be seen to make a contribution to the health education curriculum, need to know about the school's health education policy, particularly so that gestures which are generous and well-meaning do not cancel out the messages of a carefully planned curriculum programme. Imagine the scenario of the setting up of a school tuck shop, perhaps run by parents who are giving up a great deal of time to its running. Can you then allow the enterprise to undermine all the carefully taught principles of healthy eating?

No one of course, would embark on such an all-embracing review within a short time span in the school's development plan, even just before an OFSTED inspection! The grid naturally divides into sections, for example Planning, or the Hidden Curriculum, on which to focus particularly. The normal cycle of planned review and curriculum development would allow the whole process to be considered, perhaps over a series of school years. The essential point is that such a process of self-evaluation does take place, and that the whole team, staff, parents and other contributors, work together to make theirs a health-promoting school.

Inspection

All schools would be well advised to equip themselves with a current copy of the *OFSTED: Framework for the Inspection of Schools* and to use it, at the least, as part of the background reading which inevitably colours one's thinking. Certainly those sections which have to do with the quality of learning, pupils' personal development and behaviour, the quality of teaching and the quality and range of the curriculum all have direct relevance for personal, social and health education.

Within the last of these, Part 2, section 7.3(i)d makes specific mention of cross-curricular issues. The glossary in Part 6 defines the cross-curricular elements.

> These run across the whole curriculum and are not confined to one subject. They cover dimensions (e.g. equal opportunities); themes (e.g. economic and industrial understanding, health education, careers education and guidance, environmental education and citizenship); and relevant skills.

Guidance given to inspectors in Part 3 includes that for making qualitative judgements, 'a judgement of the quality of learning...including identifiable gains in knowledge, skills and understanding'; 'an assessment of the suitability of the method(s) chosen' and the identification of 'substantial references in the lesson to... cross-curricular themes'. 'A good curriculum is one which complies fully with legal requirements...includes coherent provision for the major cross-curricular themes, dimensions and skills, including personal and social education and preparation for adult life'. (Part 4 Section 7.3(i)).

Many references in the OFSTED inspection framework are of a general application and can serve to focus attention on any area of teaching, but it is obviously intended that the cross-curricular themes, such as health education, are to be given due consideration in the taught, informal and hidden curriculum. Paper 12 on Health and Safety in Section 5 makes specific reference to 'safe practice... knowledge... awareness of health and safety... teaching which helps pupils to understand... practice which gives due regard to health and safety but also challenges and stimulates good leaning experiences' and underlines the point that there are responsibilities for health education lodged in the statutory orders for some subjects. Part 2, section 4, On the Efficiency of the School, identifies evidence from 'any documentation relating to an evaluation of quality and standards in the school.' and seeks information on the provision and use of resources. The documentary evidence required includes the statutory 'policy for sex education' (Part 2 Section 7.3.(i)f) which has its natural place in a whole school health education policy. Paragraphs which define moral and social education, give guidance for the inspection of equal opportunities or how a school relates to 'the wider community' or 'practises the effective deployment of other adults' all serve to act as pointers to the observations which are likely to be seen as significant. Once embarked on the treasure hunt for references to or inferences appropriate to health education in the inspection framework, it might prove to be addictive, but it is an excellent way of supporting a school's own critical appraisal of its work.

The inspection is intended to reflect all aspects of the school's life and to observe whether and how the statutory and obligatory responsibilities are carried out. Those schools which plan thoroughly, implement faithfully and effectively, monitor efficiently and make time to review and evaluate should reap their reward in both the report of the inspection and the professional development which ought to be the outcome of such a process.

CHAPTER 11

The Health-Promoting Primary School: Key Issues for Teaching and Learning

Ron Morton

This book is concerned with raising the various issues that affect the delivery of health education and health promotion in schools, and in the primary school in particular. The health educator is literally anyone who is engaged in developing a pupil's understanding of his or her welfare requirements, how best to support those requirements and, to a certain extent, those of others. The various authors, all of them practitioners, emphasise the importance for health educators, especially those leading the way, to be aware of the issues related to the key themes of health, to be clear about what should be taught and how best to teach, or facilitate the educational process.

At the heart of the educational process lies the child, but if the process itself is lacking direction, is without intellectual rigour and devoid of purpose and vision then it fails to serve both the needs of the child and ultimately the future needs of society. If health education in schools is to achieve the task set it must develop in the young the knowledge and skills which will assist them to define and determine the quality of life that a caring and civilised society should endeavour to provide for its people. If this can be achieved then it brings a new meaning to the term, 'The Health of the Nation'.

Theoretically, the inclusion of health education as an essential part of the primary school curriculum should not require prompting, defending or promoting. Any human society that regards itself as civilised and claims to have highly developed material and spiritual resources and a complex cultural, political and legal organisation within an advanced state of social development, should not need to justify the need to address within educational provision the physical, mental and spiritual well-being of its young people. They will, after all, constitute the future well-being – or otherwise – of the society itself. In short, the inclusion of health education, indeed, its existence and prominence, within the primary school curriculum, should be viewed both as an entitlement of the young and as an investment for the future of any society.

In their discussion paper on curriculum organisation and classroom practice in primary classrooms, Alexander, Rose and Whitehead (1992) refer to:

wider concerns about whether standards achieved by primary school pupils constitute an adequate preparation for the demands of life in modern society.

This particular concern addresses educational standards, but for health education in the primary school to earn its place as a priority and entitlement within a broad and balanced (some would say over-stretched) curriculum, it has to prove that it not only shares those concerns but also could not be accused of contributing to them. However health education in the primary school is delivered, teaching and learning have to prove their credibility on the strength of their quality. Credibility will not be gained through 'preciousness' but because health education is academically and intellectually challenging, as well as contributing to the emotional and physical well-being of the child.

Whilst not wishing to be dismissive of genuinely important health goals, health education and health promotion in the primary school are about far more than meeting the Health of the Nation targets. Indeed, the key issues for health education and promotion in the primary school relate to how effective schools can be in enabling young people to develop skills and attitudes, through knowledge and experiences, that will demonstrate the true potential of health education to be the dynamic force for self-empowerment. For this, albeit lofty, ideal to have a chance of success health education must be methodically addressed within the school curriculum; must be reflected in the school's ethos; should extend to the pupil's family and community; must include the welfare of the staff; must employ the resources and expertise required and, perhaps above all, be supported by the senior management and led by the committed.

Starting Points

In her case study on initiating health policy and practice in the primary school, Danai (Chapter 8) declares that her starting point for the introduction and implementation of health education in her school was that of six critical questions first posed by Whitehead and Foster (1984), relating to identifying concerns and how to respond to them. Having defined her rationale, once in the classroom the starting point for her pupils was the 'Draw and Write' investigation technique employed by Williams, Wetton and Moon (1989). Both exercises are about discovering what is actually already understood by the term 'health' and identifying those health related activities already taking place. If planning for health education within the school and the classroom is to ensure consistency and progression then such a review is vital. Furthermore, such a 'discovery exercise' can and should involve the pupils and all those concerned, and should take into account that:

due recognition is given to the importance of first-hand experiences and practical tasks in the acquisition and application of knowledge and skills and regular opportunities are provided for children to reflect systematically upon such experiences. (NCC 1, 1989)

For schools, the 'discovery exercise' could begin with an audit, either a broad sweep of all matters regarding health and safety or by targeting a particular area. The following example of how such an audit may form the basis of a school development plan for health education, or, conversely, how a school development plan for health could form the basis for an audit, is taken from an actual primary school SDP for health as used at West Heath Junior School in Birmingham.

STAFF DEVELOPMENT PLAN – HEALTH
- Staff welfare: an entitlement to be ill without concern over cost to school;
- non-contact time guaranteed;
- regular encouragement, praise and reward;
- stress checked – workload eased when and wherever possible (to enable good teaching to take place, family/personal life to exist);
- explicit trust – i.e. go off premises when not teaching (perhaps go the bank), given task to see through without interference, etc;
- entitlement to support family needs, i.e. visit hospital for appointments, see own child's assembly;
- try to ensure job satisfaction;
- support from senior management team;
- encourage one to a feel a valued professional and colleague;
- awareness of and responsive to equal opportunities issues;
- access to workplace nursery;
- genuine career guidance given – in the interest of the employee.

CURRICULUM DEVELOPMENT PLAN – HEALTH
- Review the role of the health education co-ordinator;
- review the school's health education policy;
- ensure that health education is appropriately planned;
- ensure that health education is cross-curricular and health-specific;
- ensure health-promoting curricular activities and events;
- set appropriate health promotion targets for the year;
- establish means for monitoring and evaluating health targets;
- establish appropriate recording and assessment procedures;
- consider and implement an appropriate system of pastoral care;
- ensure this complements a policy for the management of pupil behaviour;
- operate a meaningful policy for the teaching of sex education;
- ensure the school meets OFSTED requirements for the welfare of pupils;
- meet the national policy expectations for health.

COMMUNITY DEVELOPMENT PLAN
- Prepare events for promoting health with an invitation extended to the community;
- parents' course with health dimension;
- school as a source for health information available to the community;
- family-school social occasions;
- parents-school health curriculum activities.

ENVIRONMENTAL/PREMISES DEVELOPMENT PLAN – HEALTH

- Review health and safety policy;
- safe and hygienic environment audit;
- well resourced first aid facilities;
- school meals service complies with school policy for healthy eating.

FINANCIAL/EXPENDITURE PLAN – HEALTH
- Ensure that money available reflects the needs of health promotion as defined in the targets set within the School Development Plan and Curriculum Development Plan;
- that school governors and parents are made aware of the needs, priorities and targets;
- that expenditure on health promotion is monitored;
- that appropriate pressure is applied to the LEA to ensure that it fulfils its obligations and duties to comply with aspects of health and safety that are its direct responsibility and all other areas, i.e. school kitchens, premises, etc, that it has a duty to maintain.

Should the school not have developed a policy for health education and promotion, then the above example would assist governors, staff, health professionals and possibly parents, working in partnership, to develop the framework for such a policy, and would certainly generate much discussion regarding the significance of the issues raised. To have a school policy is ultimately essential, but whether the policy comes before the practice or the practice comes before the policy will depend on how much support there is for health education, and how far the critical thinking of health educators has developed. For this purpose, it may well be necessary for the school to identify and support the in-service training requirements of its staff before it engages in creating a health policy. Note particularly the determination of the school to meet the welfare needs of the school staff. If schools really do value the staff and see them as the school's most important and costliest resource then surely it makes sense to invest in their welfare. And how can a school justifiably claim to be caring if its ethos and philosophy do not demonstrably extend to the staff?

Influences and Lifetsyles

If it is assumed that health education itself is about informing and influencing the decision making process in order to constitute empowerment within the individual, then it has to engage the very influences that could either support or undermine its aims and objectives. In a sense, health education, as part of its process, needs to investigate and challenge the validity of that which could either enable or prevent its success. Therefore it is important for health educators to examine carefully the influences on children and young people and to consider how to engage those influences in support of positive health outcomes.

For the primary school child, the family, peers, school and teachers, its environment and community, the media, culture and religion are all strong influences. Many of the child's values and attitudes will be acquired as a result of these influences. Each life experience becomes a learning experience with the potential for determining, for good or ill, the lifestyle of the child and perhaps even the adult he or she becomes.

The task for the health educator is to evaluate with the child those influences and lifestyles that are thought to be worthwhile and beneficial to good, healthy lifestyles and to compare the negative alternatives analytically, not sensationally. To achieve this it is worth taking note of NCC Guidance 1 (1989):

> pupils are led to ask questions and seek answers individually and in co-operation with others, and their thinking is guided and informed sympathetically by teachers and other adults.

By this means, health education values the knowledge and experiences that children bring to the classroom. Therefore opportunities are created that not only prevent barriers being formed but in reality offer the opportunity for learner to become teacher and teacher to become learner.

Perhaps the first lesson for the health educator is that there is nothing to be gained merely by raising issues. When that occurs, health education is only an awareness-raising exercise. Effective health education leads towards health promotion when issues are raised and solutions are sought, and when this is a developmental process for both teacher and pupil. The second important lesson is that experience shows that to condemn a particular influence or lifestyle without a feasible and convincing rationale usually proves ineffective and often counterproductive, and this is even more likely if an alternative option is denied or dismissed. Scott (Chapter 4) states that:

> Exercise, nutrition, smoking and alcohol programmes all tread this line between coercion and choice, between education and instruction, individual wants and rights and community needs.

In order to promote healthy eating, a primary school might operate a fruit-only tuck shop and make its point very effectively *without* banning the eating of sweets or crisps.

But a school has the right to promote the values and principles it believes to be in the interests of its pupils and community. If these are arrived at as a result of a consensus then so much the better. If not, then the school has to make clear not only in whose interests it is acting but also the reasons why.

The School, Family and Community

Health education begins in the home. This is an area where it is generally acknowledged that the primary school is best placed to be supportive of the home and to receive support from the home. This, as Morton (Chapter 3) indicates, is fundamentally what partnership between parents and schools is about. It is more easily developed through health education than through any other subject of the curriculum.

The reception class has much to teach the rest of the school in how best to manage and merge the influences of the home and school in the interests of the child. Pivotal to learning in the first year of schooling are the experiences the child brings to school. Reception class teachers, like the rest of their early years teaching colleagues, may extend those home-life experiences but can seldom ignore them. Instead they are utilised in order to explore teaching and learning situations. Health education in the primary school should be supportive of a child-centred, experiential approach to learning. That does not imply, as critics of such an approach often do, that the process is undemanding and the outcome is intellectually feeble. On the contrary, what is expected is that such a pedagogy begins 'where the pupil is at' and develops into what the pupil needs to know, taking into account that:

> teachers' expectations of what pupils are capable of achieving are high and pupils' learning is structured, relevant and stimulating; (NCC 1, 1989)

Health education is challenging when it is intellectually rigorous. At any age or level, good health education is that which intellectually challenges habits, practices and perceptions. Such teaching often requires sensitivity and courage, particularly when the health educators' own *mores* are threatened. Veasey - (Chapter 5) illustrates what health education demands, particularly of the educator, when discussing the issues relating to sex education in the primary school:

> Yet in spite of intense media obsession with sex, it is not a topic easily fitted into adult-child conversation. Why is it so subject to 'adult' censorship? When adults reflect on their own experience of sexuality, then check out what they *think* they know, they become aware of prejudices acquired, and peculiarities of understanding which it may be wrong or misleading to pass on. Children need to be nurtured, shown which way to go, and protected on their way to becoming sexually healthy adults.

If health education in the primary classroom does not relate to children's experiences and influences it will deny them the development of the essential powers of control over their bodies and minds that should enable them to choose good health options.

Part of the task for the health educator in the primary classroom is to challenge the myth that children and young people generally appear to believe in, which is that of their own immortality – the 'Peter Pan' syndrome – and to do so without damaging their optimism for the future. A recent school project on old age, undertaken by a West Midlands primary school, surprised teachers by how difficult the concept of ageing was for primary school children. Many found it difficult to see their own physical development as part of an ageing process. This perception of immunity from ageing and from the major illnesses and diseases, such as cancers, HIV/AIDS and coronary heart disease, is a fundamental obstacle for the health educator. A coercive dismissal of certain influences and lifestyles in favour of a prescribed alternative is not necessarily an answer likely to gain much acceptance. Yet it is vital that alternative and more beneficial lifestyles are shown to be available – and to emphasise that the responsibility lies with the individual who can, if properly informed and so choosing, be in control of making decisions conducive to her or his own good health. Above all, it is important to emphasise that this element of control lies, to a certain degree, within the power even of children in the primary school classroom who can, for example, decide how much exercise they wish to indulge in, the amount of sweets they eat, the kind of relationships they engage in, their response to peer group pressure and how they determine their personal safety.

Close relationships are a central feature of the primary school. A successful school, apart from good leadership, commitment, vision and direction, will have highly developed supportive relationships between teachers, pupils, parents and governors. The primary school can function in a health-promoting way only if, as Bruce (Chapter 6) and Wright (Chapter 7) remind us, children's feelings about themselves and each other are of paramount concern to the health-promoting primary school. This will determine not merely how a school responds within the framework of the 1989 Children Act (in relation to raising a child's awareness of their own safety), but also how a child feels about him/herself, others, and above all how she or he interacts with others and responds to the challenges life sets.

This central, perhaps even pivotal, strand of health education is not merely about character building; it is about developing attitudes and establishing values that will determine the way in which decisions are made and the kind of decisions made in relation to the welfare of the individual and others. Relationships do not just happen. In fact so important a role do they play in the success of an individual or institution that how they are created and nurtured ought to be enshrined in school policy. Not many schools actually appear to have a specific policy on 'relationships' and this might well be regarded as a serious omission.

The notion of relationships applies not just to those between children but also to those between home and school, the school and its various supporting agencies and between the teacher and pupils. For some aspects of health education in the primary school, for example sex education and the management of pupil behaviour, the health educators will need to ask searching questions of themselves, regarding their own relationship with their pupils and their own confidence and competency to deal with certain issues. In sex education this might be, 'How far am I prepared to go in responding to pupil questions?' In the management of pupil behaviour, a question might be, 'Am I the cause of this pupil's alienation? If so, why?' Teaching health education in the primary school can arguably be easier than at later stages of schooling, if only because teachers and pupils spend more time together. As a result the relationships may be better and the understanding deeper. However, it is also possible for relationships to be fragile because they (in many but not all cases) are closer. The dialogue may be less guarded and the questioning closer to the edge.

For teachers, particularly those who favour a formal teaching methodology, engaging in a more open form of dialogue can be an uncomfortable experience for both teacher and pupil, and in some cases may be disastrous. Such colleagues, as Lloyd (Chapter 9) reminds us, will need support and time to develop the skills that other teachers find it easier to acquire. It may be necessary to introduce ground rules such as limitations on what will be discussed and what will not; that matters of confidentiality will be respected; that only correct terminology will be used. These strategies are as much for the benefit of the pupil as the teacher. They may remain as a permanent fixture or be used as a temporary measure. Health educators can only develop personal esteem and self-confidence as a basis for promoting practice of good health if their own relationships with those they teach are themselves positively healthy and based on mutual respect and a degree of understanding.

The School Environment

Most primary schools take pride in presenting a creative and stimulating school environment, reflecting standards of achievement and a sense of pupil ownership. They try to ensure that the visitor to the school is received in a welcoming atmosphere and environment.

The opportunity that the school environment offers for making important statements about the ethos of the school, for communicating essential health messages and for emphasising and reinforcing vital teaching and learning points in relation to health education, should be neither underestimated nor underused.

Failure to use the environment to promote the school's commitment to health education gives the impression that health education is undervalued; that the school's policy for health education is at best theoretical and academic rather than pragmatic and applied, and that the school has failed to note the difference between being health-educating and health-promoting. Failure to use the school environment for health-promoting purposes could actually deny children an opportunity to put into practice the health skills they have acquired. Decision making is rendered irrelevant if no decisions are made. Furthermore, if empowerment is a genuine goal for health education, whereby health educators are encouraging young people to take responsibility for themselves, then it goes without saying that the exercise of empowerment requires a means of expression – which can be safely applied through the action taken within the school environment.

There is evidence that many primary school children undertake very comprehensive health and safety audits on the school environment. The effective health-promoting school takes this activity beyond that of data gathering. It encourages action plans to be devised and then supports the implementation of the plans with appropriate resources. It is the decision making and action that turns policy and theory into practice and is a process that can be shared by all concerned: the health and safety officer, governors, the school nurse and doctor, grounds maintenance company, health promotion officer, teachers, pupils and parents. Although this may not in reality happen in every aspect of health education and promotion, the school environment can lead the delivery of health promotion within the school and within the school's community.

Monitoring, Evaluation and Review

The clear guide-lines set out in National Curriculum *Guidance 5 on Health Education* indicate, as has been shown by Lloyd and Morton (1992), that at Key Stage 1 and Key Stage 2, health education can be addressed within every core and foundation subject as well as RE. Like any other subject of the curriculum, health education must prove itself by producing evidence by which it can be judged.

Muriel Phillingham (Chapter 10) states that:

> The methods of assessment of children's understanding are many and varied. Methods which reveal whether children have changed behaviour or reinforced healthy lifestyles are ultimately more worthwhile.

Health education, when taught in a cross-curricular or thematic/project context, yields a variety of evidence, both in terms of health and in terms of the core and foundation subject matter. Teachers in a busy primary classroom should seek the opportunity to derive summative, formative and evaluative assessment from the health activities taking place but should also have specific criteria by which health can be judged, and specific criteria for assessment relating to other subjects.

The evidence upon which decisions are made in health education are part of an on-going process. The school development plan shown earlier in this chapter provides a range of prompts, the response to which can enable one to gauge what has been achieved and what needs to be achieved. However, the effective school is assessed by quality of achievement. It is generally acknowledged that this is brought about through setting targets within a specific framework and judging them according to a set of success criteria. The same procedures should apply as much to health education and promotion within the school as to any other aspect of the school's curriculum.

Special Education Needs

It would be surprising if a school that made concise, accurate and meaningful assessments of its pupils' progress did not provide a good system of support for those considered to need them. Assuming that a school's additional help for pupils with identified special needs aims at integration and the prevention of alienation, its philosophy and practice will be closely allied to the school's policy for health education. This is especially so, if it is declared that a personal and social model for health education is perceived as being important. That is, it is expected that successful learning will take place for any pupil, regardless of capability, when a pupil has high self-esteem and feels confident about him/herself. This does not imply that one should 'never point out when a pupil is wrong', a caution stated by Alexander, Rose and Whitehead (1992). On the contrary, often the opposite may be necessary. But criticism has to be partnered with explanations and alternatives, with the intention of developing those skills of critical thinking and problem-solving which are essential to modifying attitudes and behaviour, and central to teaching and learning in health education.

The Curriculum

Health education, therefore, is not merely about dialogue between health educator and pupil; it is about interaction, and should involve the knowledge, experiences and expertise of all concerned, including parents and pupils. All should have an opportunity to perform in varying degrees, as teachers, facilitator, tutors, helpers and contributors. It is the interaction, using a range of organisational strategies and teaching methodologies within a planned framework, showing clear lines of progression and taking into account the identity and needs of the school and its community, that will most successfully address the health needs of pupils through the curriculum of the school.

Two key elements in the delivery of health education referred to so far are those of 'interaction' and 'partnership'. Clearly, if there is a relationship between the educators based on the notion of partnership, a consensus will be arrived at by the partners regarding matters of mutual respect, high expectations and the understanding that at any one time the lead is likely to be assumed within the partnership by whoever has the 'subject knowledge'. Alexander, Rose and Whitehead (1992) state:

> Our own view is that subject knowledge is a critical factor at every point in the teaching process; in planning, assessing and diagnosing.

However, the ownership of subject knowledge, as Morton (Chapter 3) clearly implies, is not always necessarily in the hands of teachers, but may well be possessed by others, including children. In addition, subject knowledge should not always be identified as a formal package accredited through academic qualifications. For example, accredited knowledge of a local community should be given to those who live within it and whose life experiences are derived from it. Who better qualified to lead on the matter of the community than those whose community it is?

The health-promoting primary school, according to the concept of the health-promoting school as described by the HEA (1993), is one which seeks 'the employment of specialist community services for advice and support in health matters.' There is room for this requirement regarding the level of involvement from the community to be extended even further. A school, in order to be health-promoting, needs to signal its commitment to being the managing agent for a range of sometimes common and sometimes competing community interests. It will have to maintain cohesion and sometimes provide direction, as well as be the formal channel through which services are applied for and received. In this respect, schools might better serve their wider communities if they were to combine their parents' rooms, where they exist, with a base for providing primary health care information and perhaps even services, no matter what degree of commitment the school shows concerning its willingness either to lead or at least support the health network. But the test of how influential, and perhaps how effective, the primary school can be as a health-promoting institution may well depend upon the degree of openness a school has towards its community and how committed it is to the welfare of its pupils, their families and to those living within the locality.

Since children's life experiences come from the place in which they live, learn and play, it can be argued, as it has been throughout this text, that health education and health promotion in the primary school have to identify a clear role for children in relation to their responsibility for their own well-being. The school should encourage and facilitate pupils' ability to identify things for which they can take responsibility; things they can be responsible for and things they can change. If these are seen as key questions, children can be encouraged to ask them of themselves. They might also be applied (perhaps towards the end) to each aspect of health studied, for example, at the end of a programme that focused on personal safety, growing up, personal hygiene, environmental health, feelings and emotions, or a study of medicine and drugs.

A health-promoting primary school, then, is one which demonstrates its willingness and capability to turn a policy for health education into practice. Its vision and commitment is such that it sets out to promote healthy lifestyles for its immediate and wider community and, above all, seeks to provide the individuals within those communities with the means to determine their own well-being. The school curriculum extends health education into health promotion through the overt declaration of its intentions and in so doing should fulfil all the criteria for a health-promoting school as defined by the HEA (1993) and as described by Lloyd (Chapter 1).

School Ethos

Interestingly, the HEA's concept of the health-promoting school makes no reference to 'school ethos'. Perhaps the reason for this is that 'school ethos' has an ethereal quality, is not empirical enough and is usually hard to define in terms of performance indicators. And yet all schools are judged – and keen to be judged – by the 'school's ethos'. When asked to describe, if not the ethos of the school as it is, then at least the kind of ethos the school aspires to, a typical and not unnatural response is as follows: a school which has high expectations of its pupils and cares deeply for their spiritual, physical, emotional and intellectual development; it aims to give its pupils a strong identity with, and commitment to, the school, through a declaration of shared ownership and entitlement, on condition that pupils (and staff) accept a shared responsibility, are honest and have respect for one another's views (in-so-far as they are held with regard for the personal esteem of individuals); which endeavours to put equal opportunities into practice and welcomes the involvement of teachers and parents in partnership.

At a time when state education in the United Kingdom is under a statutory requirement to render itself accountable to the public who finance it, when schools are no longer self-regulating institutions but are managed by governors directly answerable to parents and are systematically audited and inspected by government appointed agencies, the ethos of a school is a critical factor in the judgement of its success or failure. The health-promoting primary school nurtures values and attitudes appropriate to good health and develops essential life skills for children starting along the path to adulthood and its weight of responsibilities. In order to accomplish this process of personal and social development, the school must have a vision of the kind of qualities, skills and characteristics necessary for both the individual and the collective role that an individual will be required to play in society. A health-promoting primary school, close to the needs of children and working with parents and its community, will know that it is succeeding when it perceives the ethos of the school as realising expectations similar to those which have been described. The health-promoting agenda and programmes set by the school generate an ethos that, by symbiosis, enhances the work of health promotion just as the work of health promotion enhances the ethos of school.

When the potential and capability of health education and health promotion are fully understood, particularly in the primary school, and fully addressed, then it is likely that future health targets for the nation might well embrace a broader vision of health than those currently defined. It is not a romantic notion to suggest that the children of today are the decision makers of tomorrow. The failure to provide adequate health education today will determine the quality of health care required and received in the future when present health educators are likely to be in the hands of those they once taught and subject to the decisions they make.

Bibliography/References

Alexander, Rose and Whitehead (1992) *Curriculum Organisation and Class-room Practice in Primary Schools: A Discussion Paper*, DFE.

Allen, Isobel (1988) *Education in Sex and Personal Relationships*, PSI 665, Oxford.

Almond, L., and Dowling, F. (1987) *Physical Education and Health Education, Health Education in Schools*, Harper and Row, London.

Anderson, J. (1988) *Health Skills: The power to choose*, Health Education Journal, Vol. 45, HEA.

Balding, J. (1989) *We Teach Them How to Drink*, HEA Schools Health Education Unit, Exeter.

Balding, J. (1993) *Very Young People in 1992-1993*, University of Exeter, Schools Health Education Unit.

Bannister (1990) 'Listening and Learning: psychodramatic techniques with children' from NSPCC, *'Listening to Children'*, Longman.

Baric, L. (1991) *Health promoting Schools, Evaluation and Auditing*, Institute of Health Education, Vol. 20. No. 4.

Baric, L. (1992) 'Promoting Health: New approaches and developments', Journal of the Institute of Health Education, Vol. 30, No.1.

Barnardo (1992) HIV/AIDS Conference, 'Telling the Children', 14 July 1992, London, Barnardos/Wellcome Foundation Ltd.

Birmingham School Board Punishment Book. Benson Road School, Benson Road, Birmingham 1896–1960, unpublished.

Braun, D., & Combes, L. (1987) 'Preparing for Practice,' Journal of Community Education, Vol. 6, No. 2.

Brown, P. and Piper, S. (1993) 'Perpetuating the status quo; a response to Jeff French and Sue Milner,' Health Education Journal, Vol. 52, No. 4.

Canter, L. (1992) *Assertive Discipline*, Lee Canter and Associates, Santa Monica, California, USA.

Child Psychotherapy Trust (1990) *Won't They Just Grow Out Of It?* (Video).

The Consumers' Association (1993) *Check It Out!* (Magazine for young people as referred to in the *Independent*, 30.10.93, p.7, 'Pupils give top marks to friends'.)

Court (1977) *Fit for the Future*, Report of the Committee on Child Health Issues, Vol. 1 (The Court Report), HMSO.

The Daily Telegraph, 26 February 1994.

Danai, K. (1993) 'How Can I Use The Principles and Procedures of Action Research to Improve My Teaching of Health Education and Link This to the Development of a Whole School Health Education Programme?' M.A. dissertation, Coventry University, unpublished.

David, K. & Williams, T. (1987) *Health Education in Schools,* Harper & Row, London.

Dearing, R. (1993) The National Curriculum and Its Assessment; Final Report, SCAA.

DES (1977) *Health Education in Schools,* HMSO.

DES (1986) *Health Education from 5 – 16: Curriculum Matters 6,* HMSO.

DES (1991) *Science in the National Curriculum,* HMSO.

DFE (1992) *The Parents' Charter,* HMSO.

DFE (1992) *Choice and Diversity: A new framework for schools,* HMSO.

DOH (1991) *Health of the Nation* White Paper, Department of Health, HMSO.

DOH (1992) *The Health of the Nation, Key Area Handbook: Coronary Heart Disease and Stroke,* Department of Health.

DOH (1992) *The Health of the Nation and You,* Department of Health.

DOH (1993) *Key Area Handbooks. Coronary Heart Disease and Stroke; Cancers; Accidents; Mental Illness; HIV/AIDS and Sexual Health,* Health of the Nation, Department of Health, HMSO.

Donahue, J. (1991a) 'Health Education and the National Curriculum,' Health Education Journal, Vol. 50, No.1.

Donahue, J. (1991b) 'Health Education and the National Curriculum,' Journal of the Institute of Health Education, Vol. 29 No. 2.

E.C. (1989) 'Resolution of the Council of Ministers of Education, meeting within Council 23rd November, 1988, concerning health education in schools' (89/c/3/01), Official Journal of the European Commission.

Elliot, J. (1991) *Action Research for Educational Change,* Open University Press.

Ewles, L. & Simnett, I. (1991) *Promoting Health: A practical guide to health education,* Wiley Chichester.

Fitzpatrick L. (1993) *The Health Education Centre.* 'A new approach to professional support and development in Australia.' Health Promotion International, Vol. 8 No. 1.

French, J. & Milner, J. (1993) 'Should we accept the status quo?' Health Education Journal, Vol. 52 No. 3.

Fulgnum, R. (1989) *All I Really Need to Know I Learned in Kindergarten – Uncommon Thoughts on Common Things,* Grafton Books, London.

Gordon, I. J. (1969) 'Developing parent power', in Grotberg, E. (ed.) *Critical Issues in Research Related to Disadvantaged Children.,* Princeton, NJ: Educational Testing Service.

Gow, I., *et al* (1989) *Unemployment, Crime and Offenders.*

Hargreaves, D. and Hopkins, D. (1992) *The Empowered School,* Cassell, London.

Harvey, J. and Passmore, S. (1994) *School Nutrition Action Group (SNAG). A New Policy for Managing Food Information in Schools,* Birmingham Health Education Unit.

HEA (1991) *Towards a Smoke Free Generation,* HEA.

HEA (1993) *The Concept of the Health Promoting School; The European Network of Health Promoting Schools. How your school can be involved,* HEA.

HEA (1993) *A survey of health education policies in schools,* HEA.

HMI (1986) *Health Education from 5-16. Curriculum Matters 6* (HMI series), HMSO.

HMI (1989) *Personal and Social Education from 5-16. Curriculum Matters 14,* HMSO.

HMSO (1956) *Health Education: Ministry of Education Pamphlet 31,* HMSO.

HMSO (1989) *Education Reform Act.*

HMSO (1989) *The Children Act – Guidance and Regulations,* Department of Health, HMSO.

HMSO (1989) *Discipline in Schools,* Report of the Commission of Enquiry into Discipline in Schools, chaired by Lord Elton (The Elton Report), HMSO.

HMSO (1991) *Working Together Under the Children Act 1989,* Home Office, Dept. of Health, DES and Welsh Office, HMSO.

HMSO (1992) *Education (Schools) Act.*

IIMSO (1993) *Asylum and Immigration Act,* HMSO.

Hyland, T. (1988) 'Morality, Individualism and Health Education', Journal of the Institute of Health Education, Vol. 26.

Jones, S. (1988) 'The collaborative approach in health education and training', Journal of the Institute of Health Education, Vol. 26.

Kogan, M., McNay, I. and Ozga, J. (1985) *Education Policy and Values: Policy Making in Education,* Oxford University Press.

Konner, M. (1991) *Childhood,* Little Brown, London.

Lancaster, J. (1810) *The British System of Education,* British and Foreign Schools Society Archives.

Lenderyou, G. (1993) *The Primary School Workbook. Teaching Sex Education within National Curriculum,* The Family Planning Association.

Lewis, C.S. (1983) *The Four Loves,* Fontana.

Lewis, D. (1993) 'Oh for those halcyon days! A review of the development of school health education over 50 years,' Health Education Journal, Vol. 52/3, HEA.

Lloyd, J. (1990) 'Personal and Social Education in the National Curriculum,' in the manual, *Skills for the Primary School Child,* TACADE.

Lloyd, J. (1991) 'Non-Smokers Do It Without Coughing', Health Education Journal, Vol. 50. No.1, HEA.

Lloyd, J. (1994) The National Evaluation of 'Skills for the Primary School Child', TACADE/DFE.

Lloyd, J. & Morton, R. (1992) *Health Education at Key Stages 1 & 2,* Teacher's Resource Books, Blueprints Series, Stanley Thornes.

Lloyd, J. & Morton, R. (1992) Health Education INSET Resource (Free with

Health Education at Key Stage 2), Blueprints Series, Stanley Thornes.

Lloyd, J., Bennett, P. & Lawrence, T. (1994) *We've Seen People Drinking*, National Primary Centre/Portman Group.

Lomax, P. (1990) An Action Research Approach to Developing Staff in Schools, BERA Dialogues No. 3. Clevedon, Multi-lingual Matters.

MacDonald, I. (1991) *Immigration Law and Practice, Third Edition*, Butterworth.

McKee, D. (1980) *Not Now, Bernard*, Andersen Press.

Mills, J. (1993) *Sexwords*, Penguin, London.

Mosley, J. *Turn your School Round*, LDA.

Moss, A.W. *Valiant Crusade – the History of the RSPCA*, Cassell, London.

My Body (1991) *My Body Project* HEA/Heinemann.

Nias, J., Southworth, G., Yeomans, R. (1988) *Primary School Staff Relationships*, ESCR Research Project.

NCC (1989) *Curriculum Guidance 1: A Framework for the Primary Curriculum*.

NCC (1990a) *Curriculum Guidance 3: The Whole Curriculum*.

NCC (1990b) *Curriculum Guidance 5: Health Education*.

NICC (1990) *Cross Curricular Themes*, Northern Ireland Curriculum Council.

NPC (1990) *Practice to Share: The Management of Children's Behaviour Needs*, National Primary Centre.

NPC (1993) *Practice to Share 2: The Management of Children's Behaviour Needs*, National Primary Centre.

O'Donnell, T. & Taylor, J. (1990) 'The Health Promoting College: An Agenda for the 1990s,' Unpublished draft, HEA, 1990. Published as *The Health Promoting College*, O'Donnell, T. & Gray, G., HEA.

OFSTED (1993) *The Framework for the Inspection of Schools*.

OFSTED (1993) *Curriculum Organization and Classroom Practice in Primary Schools: A follow up report*.

Phillingham, M. (1993) Lincolnshire County Council Support Materials: *Cross Curricular Themes; Health Education*.

Pugh, G. (1989) 'Pre-school Services: Is Partnership Possible?' in Wolfendale, S. (ed.) *Parental Involvement*, Cassells Educational Ltd.

Richard, D. (1990) *Has Sex Education failed our teenagers?* Focus on the Family Publishing, Carolina.

Rodnell, S. (1986) *The Policies of Health Education – Raising the Issues*, Routledge, London.

Rogers, C. (1983) *Freedom to Learn* (Revised Edition), Merril, New York.

Ross, T. (1989) *I'm Coming to Get You*, Andersen Press.

Rudduck, J. (1991) *Innovation and Change*, Buckingham, Open University Press.

Sanders, P. & Swindon, L. (1990) *Knowing me Knowing You; Strategies for Sex Education in the Primary School*, LDA.

Sayer, J. (1989) 'Facing Issues in Parents' Responsibility for Education,' in Wolfendale, S. (ed.) *Parental Involvement*, Cassells.

Sleap, M. & Perch, S. (1989) *Happy Heart 1* HEA/Nelson.

Sleap, M. & Warburton, P. (1989) *Happy Heart 2* HEA/Nelson.

Smith, C., Roberts, C., Nutbeam, D. & McDonald G. (1992) 'A Survey in 87 schools by Health Promotion Wales', in 'The Health Promoting School', *Health Promotion International*, Vol. 7 No. 3 p.171.

Scott P. (1992) 'Accountability, Responsiveness and Responsibility', in *Educational Institutes and their Environments: Managing the Boundaries,* (ed.) Glatter, R. Open University Press.

TACADE (1990) *Skills for the Primary School Child.*

Tannahill, A. (1994) 'Health Education as Health Promotion: From Priorities to Programmes,' Health Education Board for Scotland.

Thomson, R. (ed.) (1993) 'Religion Ethnicity,' in *Sex Education: Exploring Issues,* Sex Education Forum, National Children's Bureau, London.

Tones, K. (1989) 'Health Education in England. An Overview', in *Health Education World Year Book of Education,* eds. James C., Balding Jr., Harris D., Kogan Page/Nichols Publishing.

Tones, K. (1990) 'The Power to Choose, Health Education and the New Public Health.' Journal of the Institute of Health Education Vol. 28 No 3.

Tones, K. (1993) 'Changing Theory and Practice: trends in methods, strategies and settings in health education'. Health Education Journal Vol. 52 No 3.

Townsend, P. & Davidson, N. (1982) *Inequalities in Health. The Black Report,* Penguin.

Turner (1964) *All Heaven in a Rage,* Michael Joseph, London.

Unicef (1989) The Convention on the Rights of the Child, adopted by the General Assembly of the United Nations, 20. 11. 89, published in Geneva: *Defence for Children,* Internation/UNICEF.

Veasey, D.J. (1993) (1) 'Sex Education from a Biblical Perspective', *Leader,* March/April.

Veasey, D.J. (1993) (2) 'Counselling for Development through Personal and Social Education: Values, Qualities and Accountability, with special reference to sex education.' Counselling: Vol. 4 No. 2 pp 106 – 108.

Ward, C. (1991) *The Dragon's Breath: A Creative Approach to Smoking Issues for Ages 7 to 13,* Birmingham LEA Health Education Unit.

Warnock, M. (1978) *Special Educational Needs,* London: HMSO.

Wellings, K. *et al.* (1994) *Sexual Behaviour in Britain* (Based on the National Survey of Sexual Attitudes and Lifestyles, funded by the Wellcome Trust.) Penguin, London.

Went, D. (1988) 'Sex Education' *Westminster Studies in Education:* Volume 11.

White, M. (1992) *Self Esteem: Its Meaning and Value in Schools,* Daniels Publishing.

Whitehead, J. (1988) *The Health Divide; Inequalities in Health in the 1980s,* Penguin.

Whitehead, J. & Foster, D. (1984) 'Action Research and Professional Development,' C.A.R.N. Bulletin No.6.

WHO (1984) *Health Promotion; a discussion document on the concepts and principles* World Health Organisation, Geneva.

148

WHO (1985) *Targets for Health for All 2000,* World Health Organisation, Copenhagen.

WHO (1990) *Healthy City Project* World Health Organisation.

WHO (1991) World Health Organisation Planning Meeting on the Health Promoting School Concept, World Health Organisation, Copenhagen.

Williams, T. (1985) 'Health Education and the School Community Interface: Towards a model of school community interaction: A School View,' in *New Directions in Health Education,* (ed.) Campbell, G., Falmer Press.

Williams, T., Wetton, N. & Moon, A. (1989) *A Picture of Health. What Makes and Keeps You Healthy?* HEA.

Williams, T., Wetton N. & Moon A. (1989) *Health for Life 1 and 2,* HEA.

Wolfendale, S. (1983) *Parental Participation in Children's Development and Education,* Gordon and Breach, London.

Wragg, T. (1991) 'Shape up for some body work', Primary Forum, *Times Educational Supplement,* 6 December 1991

Young, I. & Whitehead, M. (1993) 'Back to the Future', *Health Education Journal* Vol. 52, No. 3, HEA.

Index